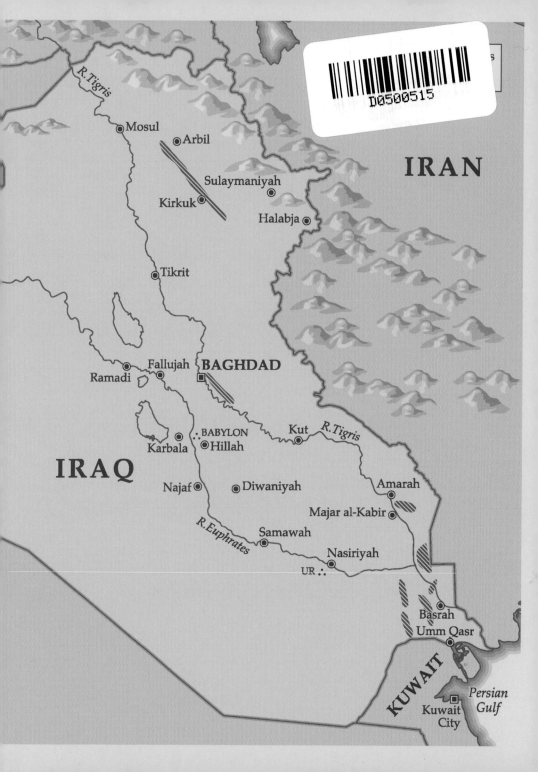

Bush in Babylon

By the same author

Bush in Babylon
The Recolonisation of Iraq

TARIQ ALI

VERSO
London • New York

First published by Verso 2003
© Tariq Ali 2003
All rights reserved

3 5 7 9 10 8 6 4 2

Verso
UK: 6 Meard Street, London W1F 0EG
USA: 180 Varick Street, New York, NY 10014-4606
www.versobooks.com

Verso is the imprint of New Left Books

ISBN 1–85984–583–5

ISBN 1–85984–536–3 (Australian paperback)

British Library Cataloguing in Publication Data
A catalogue record for this book is available from the British Library

Library of Congress Cataloging-in-Publication Data
Ali, Tariq.
    Bush in Babylon: the recolonisation of Iraq / Tariq Ali. – 1st ed.
    p. cm.
    Includes index.
    ISBN 1-85984-583-5
    1. Iraq War, 2003. 2. Iraq War, 2003–Occupied territories.
    3. United States–Relations–Iraq. 4. Iraq–Relations–United States.
    I. Title.

    DS79.76.A39 2003
    956.7044´3–dc22
                                                            2003017638

Typeset in Bembo
Printed and bound in the USA by R.R. Donnelley & Sons
Printed and bound in the UK by Bath Press
Printed and bound in Australia by Griffin Press

*For Aisha and her comrades –
a new generation on the march.*

Contents

ACKNOWLEDGEMENTS

On the first anniversary of the attacks on the Pentagon and Twin Towers it was already clear that the Bush administration was preparing to invade and occupy Iraq. I had, of course, followed the First Gulf War and written at length against the sanctions that followed, both in the *New Left Review* and *The Clash of Fundamentalisms*. Now I began to think seriously of the tortured history of this country and wanted to go back to the roots. My Lebanese friend and comrade for over thirty years, Gilbert Achcar, advised me to take a deep breath, find some spare time and read Hanna Batatu's classic study of Iraq. It was excellent advice. Reading Batatu is a rare privilege. This was a historian with a unique vision and his work travelled with me on long plane journeys to almost every continent.

I moved on to numerous other books, some of which were highly entertaining (memoirs of early British ambassadors, Gertrude Bell's diaries, etc.), and lengthy conversations with Iraqi exiles, but always returning to Batatu to check a historical fact and his interpretation of it. He did not live to see the recolonisation of Iraq, but would have hated every moment of it, especially the crude manufacturing of images: Saddam's statue pulled down by two hundred people and American equipment, in a Baghdad where there are over a million Kurds, presented as a 'liberating experience' by the propaganda machinery of the occupation.

ACKNOWLEDGEMENTS

Or the completely faked story of Private Jessica Lynch's heroism. Or the outright lies told by Bush and Blair to convince their own citizens. But Batatu died in 2000, leaving all those who have learnt from him greatly in his debt.

The Iraqis who spoke with me and helped in various ways are too numerous to list and some might prefer not to be mentioned lest they are put on the prohibited list of the occupation. But some names must be mentioned: Saadi Youssef, Haifa Zangana, Kamil Mehdi, Amir al-Rikaby, Wadood Hammad, Najim Mahmood, Faris Wahhab all spent valuable time to discuss the past. The last mentioned translated some crucial passages from Arabic for this book. Tareq Ismail in Calgary kindly sent me the relevant chapters from his forthcoming 'History of Iraqi Communism'. Many thanks to Sarah Maguire and Hafiz Kheiri for stepping in to ensure that the latest poems of Saadi Youssef and Mudhaffar al-Nawab were translated in time for publication.

At Verso HQ in London, Jane Hindle, Tim Clark, Gavin Everall, Fiona Price and Peter Hinton ensured a smooth production. Andrea Woodman and Alice McNeill haggled intensively to ensure we got most of the photographs from the old days and Andrea Stimpson did the typesetting. In the New York office Niels Hooper and Rachel Guidera chased after the image which finally became the cover. Verso takes a great deal of care to ensure that its covers are both iconoclastic and stylish, something much easier to do if you're an independent publisher who is prepared to buck the market and prove it wrong.

Tariq Ali
15 July 2003

1

INTRODUCTION: LIVING WITH THE ENEMY

Why are otherwise intelligent people in Britain and the United States surprised on learning that the occupation is detested by a majority of Iraqi citizens?[1] Could the reason be that there is no memory of being occupied in these two countries, notwithstanding the Roman conquest of Britain? Even in the latter case, there was episodic resistance of which Agricola, the most gifted Roman proconsul in Britain, was informed soon after his arrival. It was not that the stinking natives were unaware of the merits of Roman civilization. It was simply that they did not like being ruled by another power. In his essay on Agricola, the Roman historian Tacitus provides a vivid description of the imperial mentality. On one of his visits to the outer reaches of the island, Agricola looked in the direction of Ireland and asked a colleague why it remained unoccupied. Because, came the reply, it consisted of uncultivable bog lands and was inhabited by wild and very primitive tribes. What could it possibly have to

---

1 Even the official Kurdish weathercocks are becoming nervous at how it might all end. They have some experience in this regard. Having, in the past, accepted largesse from Israelis, the Shah of Iran, Ayatollah Khomeini, and various regimes in Baghdad and the US, their fine-tuned antennae can detect the smallest change in the political atmosphere. Could the new colonial regime mean that the special privileges they enjoyed from the West, while the rest of Iraq was slowly throttled, are coming to an end?

offer the great Empire? The unfortunate man was sternly admonished. Economic gain isn't all. Far more important is the example provided by an unoccupied country. It may be backward, but it's still free.

Continental Europeans and Russians have more recent experience of the phenomenon and of what it provokes – a resistance on many different levels. The plea to the Iraqis not to fight back or resist the Anglo-American occupation – coming as it did from French Gaullists, German Greens/social-democrats, the Russian oligarchy and numerous European others – struck a strange note. Was it simply Northern arrogance with regard to the South; or a desire to appease the United States; or a belief that Iraqis are a different or lower breed of people who might be happier under occupation, just like the Palestinians? Perhaps it was a mixture of all three. Whatever the reason, the Iraqis appear to have ignored the pleas.

Empires sometimes forget who they are crusading against and why, but the occupied rarely suffer from such confusions. During the first colonisation of Iraq a special elite layer was created by the British to help sustain imperial rule in the country. This was after the First World War, during which Britain fought the decaying Ottoman Empire for mastery of Mesopotamia, suffering one major defeat and several minor setbacks in the process, with colonial troops from India taking heavy casualties on each occasion.

It was the underprivileged social layers in the cities who led the resistance during the inter-war years. The reports currently coming out of Baghdad and Basrah suggest that, while the merchants and traders are prepared to live with the occupation, it is the poor, above all, who regard it as a national indignity. And if the illegal plans being hatched by Viceroy Bremer to sell off Iraqi oil in perpetuity to foreign exploiters – in order to pay for the enormous costs of the war and the occupation – come to fruition, then even the merchant classes will begin to grumble. Few

Iraqis, apart from Ahmed Chalabi and his cronies, would like to lose control of their oil. If a referendum on this question alone were permitted, over 90 percent of the population would vote for Iraqi control of Iraqi oil.

But this is imperialism in the epoch of neo-liberal economics. Everything will be privatised, including civil society. Like aliens from another planet, once the cities are secured (if that ever happens), NGOs will descend on Iraq like a swarm of locusts and interbreed with the locals. Intellectuals and activists of every stripe in all the major cities will be bought off and put to work producing bad pamphlets on subjects of purely academic interest. This has the effect of neutering potential opposition or, to be more precise, of confiscating dissent in order to channel it in a safe direction. The message from the donors is straightforward: make some noise, by all means, but if you do anything really political that seriously affects the functioning of the neo-liberal state on any level, your funds might not be renewed. And, as usually happens, participation in serious politics is likely to be forbidden. This is then characterised as 'civil society' or 'real grass-roots democracy', cleaner and more user-friendly than any political party. Users may be limited, but the NGO salaries from the West are there to ensure that this remains the case. Some NGOs do buck the trend and are involved in serious projects, but these are an exception. Long-term experiments in Egypt and Pakistan have produced reasonable results. The main problem in both places is that religious groups have seized the day, filled the vacuum, and argued against consumerism as the dominant value in contemporary societies. There is no effective secular opposition in either country, both of which are presided over by military dictators.

Elsewhere military regimes have been gently eased out of existence and replaced with a new form of rule. Capitalist democracy = privatisation + 'civil society'. This tried-and-tested formula has already wrecked much of Latin America and the whole of Africa. The dictatorship of capital is proving much more resilient than the military variety. It now threatens to roll over Iraq. Will it succeed?

The occupation is still in its infancy. Its aims are simple: to impose privatisation and a pro-Western regime in Iraq. But its ability to do so permanently is circumscribed by the history and consciousness of the Iraqi people. This is not to imply that the whole country is desperate for a protracted war. If anything, the opposite is the case. If the occupation succeeds in stabilising the country, and if basic amenities are restored together with some semblance of normality, then a Vichy-style operation staffed by local jackals could succeed, if only for a limited period. There are a few spunky little jackals, evil-tempered to those who do not share their vision of the occupation as 'liberation', but politically quite agile despite the fact that they have nil support in the country. They tell Bremer that as long as Saddam Hussein is alive, people think he might stage a come-back and, therefore, support for the occupation will remain restricted. The imperialist *fatwa* against Saddam includes a $25m reward for his assassination. Presumably this item of expenditure, like the bounty paid for killing Saddam's two sons and a grandson, will be paid for out of the proceeds of Iraqi oil.

But none of this is feasible so long as there is an armed resistance. While the Ba'athists dominate this resistance in the Baghdad region, they are not the only people involved and Western reporters have acknowledged that there is a near-universal rejoicing in private when an occupation soldier is killed. And if there is no early resolution to the conflict we could see the emergence of a much broader national resistance, as other organisations begin to worry that the Ba'athists, through having played a leading role in the struggle, may restore their credibility amongst significant sectors of the population. Were the Iraqi Communist Party, a section of the Kurdish organisations and the Shia to take such a plunge, it would become virtually impossible for the United States to hold on to Iraq indefinitely.

If the situation in the Baghdad region remains turbulent and the Shia hierarchy refuses to do a 'serious' deal with Bremer – that is, to cave in completely – the United States might have no option but to opt for a rapid Balkanisation. This would mean redrawing the lines in the sand that created the country and producing three protectorates, modelled on the old Ottoman *vilayets* of Baghdad, Basrah and Mosul. In effect, this would mean a Kurdish entity controlling the oil and would doom the region to ugly civil wars and ethnic cleansing. There are two million Kurdish people living in Baghdad. Genuine humanitarian considerations rarely bother imperial politicians and, for that reason, they might consider the protectorate possibility as offering the safest medium-term solution. The current division of the country into three regions has created the possibility of a de facto partition of Iraq. If Kerbela became the capital of an Islamic republic in the South, it would undoubtedly aim to reach a security agreement with the Islamic republic of Iran. Could the Empire tolerate such an affront? And would the Turkish military leave the Kurdish entity alone, or would it have to become an Israeli protectorate like Jordan? And what of Baghdad? Back to the Ba'ath? It could happen unless new opposition forces emerge.

It is the children of occupied or war-torn countries who find it difficult and painful to accept an alien presence, which is creating enormous problems for their parents. In 1857, during the first large uprising against the British in India, children became willing, eager and courageous couriers, carrying messages to neighbouring villages. When, in the late 1950s and early 1960s, an Algerian national movement erupted to confront the settlers and their patrons, children, including those between eight and ten years of age, played an active part. During a visit to Hanoi in 1966, at the height of the US bombing raids on North Vietnam, I remember finding the city strange and spooky. And then I realised why this was so. There were no children. They had all been evacuated, in most cases against their will. It

Nizar Qabbani.

was not till I visited villages in the interior that I saw any children. Their teachers complained bitterly that they refused to study in the makeshift schools created in caves and underground shelters. The only way the children could be persuaded to study was by the promise that their homework would be marked in downed US planes and helicopters. That worked. Palestinian teachers have used Israeli tanks and stones to good effect.

In recent years children have been at the forefront of resistance in Palestine. The Syrian poet Nizar Qabbani called them the 'children of the stones', applauding their courage and telling them to ignore the moth-eaten leaders of the Arab world who had always betrayed them. In 'I Am With Terrorism', one of his last political poems, written a year before his death in 1998, he turned the label of 'terrorism' against those who used it to justify tyranny and occupation. The 'terrorism' that Qabbani is identifying with is not that of 9/11 or of random bombings and killings. His own wife Balquis al-Rawi was killed when pro-Iranian mujahideen in Lebanon bombed the Iraqi embassy during the Iraq–Iran war. The poet had gone out to buy newspapers. When he returned his much-loved partner lay dead. He remembered her in numerous poems. The tragedy marked the rest of his life. Her memory haunted him till he died. And so for this poet, 'terrorism' is the word used by oppressors to defame a national liberation struggle. He would not allow this and wrote a message in a bottle to the youth of Palestine and an Arab nation that had forgotten its name:

> We are accused of terrorism:
> if we defend the rose and a woman
> and the mighty verse …
> and the blueness of sky …
> A dominion … nothing left therein …
> No water, no air …
> No tent, no camel,
> and not even dark Arabica coffee!!
> …
> We are accused of terrorism:
> if we write of a ruined homeland the ruins of a homeland
> torn, weak …
> a homeland without an address
> and a nation with no name.
> …
> A homeland forbidding us from buying a newspaper
> or listening to the news.
> A dominion where birds are forbidden
> from chirping.
> A homeland where, out of terror,
> its writers became accustomed to writing about
> nothing.
> A homeland, in the likeness of poetry in our lands:
> It is vain talk,
> no rhythm,
> imported

Ajam, with a crooked face and tongue:
No beginning
No end
No relation to the concerns of the people
mother earth
and the crisis of humanity.

...

A dominion ...
going to peace talks
with no honor
no shoe.

...

A homeland,
men piss in their pants ...
women are left to defend honor.

...

Salt in our eyes
Salt in our lips
Salt in our words
Can the self carry such dryness?
An inheritance we got from the barren Qahtan?
In our nation, no Mu'awiya, and no Abu Sufiyan
No one is left to say 'NO'
and face the scurriers
they gave up our houses, our bread and our [olive] oil.
They transformed our bright history into a mediocre store.

...

In our lives, no poem is left,
since we lost our chastity in the bed of the Sultan.

...

8

They got accustomed to us, the humbled.
What is left to man
when all that remains
is disgrace?
...
I seek in the books of history
Ussamah ibn al-Munqith
Uqba ibn Nafi'
Omar, and Hamzah
and Khalid, driving his flocks conquering the Shem.
I seek a Mu'tasim Billah
Saving women from the cruelty of rape
and the fire.
...
I seek latter day men
All I see is frightened cats
Scared for their own souls, from
the sultanship of mice.
...
Is this an overwhelming national blindness?
Are we blind to colors?
...
We are accused of terrorism
If we refuse to die
with Israel's bulldozers
tearing our land
tearing our history
tearing our Evangelium
tearing our Koran
tearing the graves of our prophets

If this was our sin,
then, lo, how beautiful terrorism is?
…
We are accused of terrorism
if we refused to be effaced
by the hands of the Mongols, Jews and Barbarians
if we throw a stone
at the glass of the Security Council
after the Caesar of Caesars grabbed it for his own.
We are accused of terrorism
if we refuse to negotiate with the wolf
and shake hands with a whore.
…
America
Against the cultures of the peoples
with no culture
Against the civilizations of the civilized
with no civilization
America
a mighty edifice
with no walls!
…
We are accused of terrorism
if we defended our land
and the honor of dust
if we revolted against the rape of people
and our rape
if we defended the last palm trees in our desert
the last stars in our sky
the last syllabi of our names

the last milk in our mothers' bosoms.
If this was our sin
how beautiful is terrorism.

…

I am with terrorism
if it is able to save me
from the immigrants from Russia
Romania, Hungary, and Poland.

…

They settled in Palestine
set foot on our shoulders
to steal the minarets of al-Quds
and the door of Aqsa
to steal the arabesques
and the domes.

…

Yesteryear
The nationalist street was fervent
like a wild horse.
The rivers were abundant with the spirit of youth.

…

But after Oslo,
we no longer had teeth:
we are now a blind and lost people.

…

We are accused of terrorism:
if we defended with full force
our poetic heritage
our national wall
our rosy civilisation

the culture of flutes in our mountains
and the mirrors displaying blackened eyes.
…
I am with terrorism
if it is able to free a people
from tyrants and tyranny
if it is able to save man from the cruelty of man
to return the lemon, the olive tree,
and the bird to the South of Lebanon
and the smile back to Golan.
…
I am with terrorism
if it will save me
from the Caesar of Yehuda
and the Caesar of Rome.
…
I am with terrorism
as long as this new world order
is shared
between America and Israel
half–half.
…
I am with terrorism
with all my poetry
with all my words
and all my teeth
as long as this new world
is in the hands of a butcher.
…
I am with terrorism

if the US Senate
enacts judgement
decrees reward and punishment.
…
I am with Irhab [terrorism]
as long this new world order
hates the smell of Arab.
…
I am with terrorism
as long as the new world order
wants to slaughter my offspring
and send them to dogs.
For all this
I raise my voice high:
I am with terrorism
I am with terrorism
I am with terrorism …

London, 15 April 1997

By making Ariel Sharon a co-leader in the 'war against terrorism', the regime in Washington consciously blurred the distinctions between national liberation and terror. The result has been catastrophic. Not a day passes without an e-mail from Israel and Palestine informing me of the latest atrocity. The material on my computer would fill two large volumes if it were presented as evidence before a war crimes tribunal. One of these e-mails arrived on 9 July 2003 and is less typical because no young children were killed. It was sent to me by Palestinian monitors:

In the early hours of this morning Israeli Special Forces and soldiers entered the West Bank town of Burkin, killing one man, seriously injuring his wife and arresting another Palestinian man. The Israeli army claims that they were fired upon when entering the village, so they returned fire, however according to Palestinian witnesses this is not true.

'The troops entered the village and went to the house next door to ours. My wife and I were sleeping on our roof when suddenly we heard some shots. We immediately entered our house. The shooting ended as soon as it began – only about four shots were fired. About 10 minutes later our door bell rang and it was Iyad and his wife. They had crawled to our front door, covered in blood and still bleeding. We called for an ambulance, and eventually it came. The medics said the soldiers had stopped them for only about 10 minutes.

'We went over and spoke to Iyad's father to see what had happened and he told us the soldiers had entered his house and arrested his 20-year-old son Fadi. Iyad, his other son, and Khaloud, Iyad's wife, and their three children, were sleeping on a bed in the garden as it was too hot in the house. When the soldiers left after arresting Fadi they must have seen them and opened fire. There was no shooting from the Palestinians – just the Israelis. We saw the mattress where the couple had been sleeping and it too was covered with blood.'

Iyad later died, according to the doctors at Rafidiya hospital in Nablus, from bullets to his throat and arms. Khaloud was shot in the face, and is currently in hospital in a critical but stable condition; their children, the eldest of whom is five years old, escaped uninjured.

With this going on every single day since 9/11 how can any thinking person be surprised that young kids are desperate to join one of the militant organisations resisting the Israelis. There is a purity and moral integrity in children that illuminates a struggle. A single hair on their head is worth more than all those who sit in judgement on them, let alone their killers.

REUTERS/POOL/Stefan Rousseau

'One of the most nauseating images of the Iraqi war was of Tony Blair kissing an Iraqi boy. What he was not kissing was the dismembered corpse of an Iraqi child, or the mutilated body of another.'

Harold Pinter

Kate Holt

Dr Assid examines a young boy admitted to Nasiriyah hospital after a cluster bomb he was playing with exploded. The hospital does not have the drugs or facilities to treat the continuing number of cases.

REUTERS/Aladin Abdel Naby

Brutal mimicry: like the Israeli army in Palestine, a US army digger destroys one of several houses in the Iraqi town of Ramadi, some 90 km (55 miles) west of Baghdad. Colonial operations of this sort have strengthened the resistance.

What will the five-year-old who escaped the bullets this time think as he grows up and hears how his father was killed and his mother defaced? Or will he not be allowed to reach that stage? Could that be the reason that the Israeli Defence Force targets young children? Are they killing future 'terrorists'? Or is it the Israeli military's homage to Malthus? That these are accidents is simply not credible any longer. It is a systematic attempt to destroy the Palestinians as a political force. And the United States is complicit in all this and indifferent to Palestinian suffering. Europe is too guilt-ridden to speak up against the perpetrators of these crimes. Incapable of acting themselves, the leaders of Western civilisation want to manacle the Palestinians so that they can't even defend themselves.

And a similar situation is now developing in parts of Iraq. US soldiers are bulldozing houses to punish whole families whose sons or father are suspected of belonging to the resistance. Photographs of young boys, their arms tied behind their backs while being interrogated by US soldiers, are reminiscent of Palestine. Carefully selected children being kissed by visiting Western politicians reminds one of the colonial period. Need one ask how Iraqi children are taking to the occupation? Every report from the country and personal messages from Iraqi friends inform one that the children of the poor quarters of the Mesopotamian cities are taunting the occupiers every day, expressing with a smile what their parents and elders whisper to each other in private. These children, now forced to spend their formative years under a foreign occupation, will be the ones who will organise a new *intifada* in the not too distant future.

This book combines Iraqi and Arab history and world politics. Without knowing the past it is impossible to understand what is happening today, and the history is presented here as a warning to both occupier and resister. The occupier will learn from it that Iraq has a very rich history of struggle against empire. The resister will, I hope, avoid the mistakes and not repeat the tragedies that permitted the occupation to happen. I am not one of those who believe that every single disaster that has befallen the Arab world is a result of Western intervention. Often the West has utilised Arab weaknesses to score victories. The self-inflicted wounds of the Arab world are discussed at length in this book because without understanding their causes it will be difficult to move forward again. The Iraqi communist leader hanged by the jackals of yesteryear in 1948 used to speak of a Free Iraq and a Happy People. Except for the year 1958, freedom and happiness were not destined to co-exist in Iraq. A new phase has now opened up in the country's history. If the old mistakes are repeated the enemy will walk through our weaknesses like ants.

2

THE JACKALS' WEDDING

Sometimes, as they contemplate the world, poets are overwhelmed by a premonition of darkness. In a letter to a friend, Rimbaud explained that to be a poet 'it is necessary to be a seer, to make oneself a seer. The poet makes himself a seer by a long, immense and reasoned unruliness of the senses ... he attains the unknown.' But it is not the senses alone or the interplay between thought and feeling that produces a seer. It is an awareness of the environment, the soil that has fertilised the thought.

During the summer of 1823, a year before the Prussian state instituted discriminatory laws to prevent Jews from teaching at schools and universities, Heinrich Heine (who would later convert from Judaism to Protestantism) wrote to a friend that he would vigorously defend the civil rights of the Jews 'and in the hard times that are sure to come the Germanic mob will hear my voice and responses will be roared in German beer halls and mansions'.

Poets with an understanding of history are often filled with a deep foreboding. They never allow themselves to become submerged in despair; they continue to hope, while recalling misdemeanours from the past as a caution to the criminals of today; they alert their readers to the punishments that befall those who remain silent and become accessories to murder. The Hebrew poet Aharon Shabtai appeals to his fellow countrymen not to think of the past only from the perspective of the oppressed, but to look inside themselves and ask if they have, even subconsciously, inherited something from their oppressors. History is unpredictable. The colonial horrors being inflicted on the Palestinians might one day confront Israelis in the dock:

> And when it's all over,
> My dear, dear reader,
> On which benches will we have to sit,
> Those of us who shouted 'Death to the Arabs!'
> And those who claimed they 'didn't know'?[2]

For most of the twentieth century, poetry – if not the poets – enjoyed considerable freedom in the Arab world, regardless of who ruled there. How did this happen? Easily learnt, it could be recited in a café; it could be recorded as songs; it could cross any frontier, travelling from city to city without fear. And this it did, helping to relieve the intellectual and spiritual hunger of the Arab nation. As for the poets, they suffered. Their lives were ruled by forced departures, by undesired exile. Once public truth is outlawed, the hour of the timeserver arrives – the jackal poet (or journalist or intellectual) who decorates official platforms, mocks all notions of the poet-as-tribune, mouths only the virtues of the intellectual-as-entertainer. But dictators, even the less intelligent ones, prefer the real thing. They are contemptuous of the jackals who can be bought and sold by the Mukhabarat (secret police) of any country.

The leader who wields absolute power (and sometimes this can be an elected politician without an opposition) believes s/he also possesses absolute wisdom and, naturally, absolute goodness and, consequently,

---

2 'Nostalgia', in *J'Accuse*, by Aharon Shabtai, New York, 2003.

s/he wants the poets who are respected by the people to write verses that deify him and honour his regime. During the early 1930s, Osip Mandelstam felt obliged to write a few very bad poems honouring Stalin. He knew they were awful. A self-cleansing antidote became necessary. Mandelstam composed a single luminous, vicious anti-Stalin poem, which he would recite only amongst close friends and even then in a whisper. But this great poet forgot (or perhaps he did not) that once a poem has escaped its confines – the poet's head – and has been written or recited, there is no way to call it back. And, tragically for Mandelstam, his poem could not be recalled. It travelled all over the old Soviet Union, translated into local languages as it chugged through the Ukraine, Georgia, Azerbaijan, and Uzbekistan. And one day Stalin heard of it and the poem arrived at the Kremlin. Once a minor poet himself and now an obsessive, Stalin must have read it many times, wondering how it was being received in the country at large and, more importantly, whether it had caused any of his Politburo colleagues to giggle while his back was turned. The poem became immortal, but it cost the poet his life.[3]

Iraq has always been a proud country. This pride has often been reflected in the work of its stubborn and steadfast poets, who refuse to bend the knee. Later in this book, I will attempt a synopsis of Iraqi history, which might help the innocent and the wicked to contextualise the outright hostility to the latest imperial occupation. But first a few words on its poets. In 1979, the year Saddam Hussein became the absolute ruler

---

3 Boris Pasternak later recalled how Stalin had rung him to ask whether it was true that Mandelstam was a 'great poet'. Pasternak claims he replied in the affirmative. By that time life in the camps had already destroyed Mandelstam's health. It was too late either to save his life or to order his execution. Pasternak himself survived the bad times. It was rumoured that the only thing that kept him safe was a review of the poetry of Georgia he had published in a literary magazine several years before the Revolution of 1917. In this review he had praised one of the Georgian poets – Joseph Djugashvili (Stalin's real name) – as showing considerable promise. Another example, perhaps, of the premonitory power that exists in great poets.

and decided to wipe out the remnants of the Left in Iraq, the poet Saadi Youssef, not wanting to write bad poems, fled Baghdad. It was impossible to make peace with the new Inquisition and remain creative. So he bade farewell to Baghdad and Basrah and sought refuge in Beirut. In April of that same year he wrote 'Friendship' and dedicated it to his friend and fellow poet Adonis:

> A quarter of a century since then
> And we arrive to find
> That Ibn Tammiya[4] has become
> The head of a bludgeon
> And al-Muwafaq[5] is still cleaving
> Rebellious slaves
> From the womb of the earth.
> The police of Damascus kick us
> And the police of Iraq
> And the Arabs' American police
> And the English
> And the French
> And the Persian
> And the Ottoman police

---

4 Ibn Tammiya (1263–1328) was a leading Sunni theologian and scholar of the Hanbali school, which was known for its ultra-orthodox interpretations of the texts. It was his ideas that were used and developed in the late eighteenth century by Abdal Wahhab and are the foundations of Wahhabism, the state religion of Saudi Arabia.

5 The reference is to the son of the Caliph al-Mutawakkil. Al-Muwafaq became the Regent during his brother's reign and acquired a reputation as the most ruthless Abbasid military commander. It was he who crushed the slave revolt in the southern marshes of Iraq. The revolt of the Zanj, an epic struggle without precedent in the annals of slavery, lasted fourteen years (869–883) till it was savagely crushed by al-Muwafaq. Many of its leaders were publicly flogged and executed in Basrah.

Saadi Youssef.

And the police of the Fatimid Caliphs [...]
Our families
Kick us,
Our naïve, good-hearted families,
Our murderous families.
We are the children of this madness.
Let's be whatever we wish.[6]

The week Baghdad fell, I rang Saadi Youssef to suggest a meeting and, if he was agreeable, lunch. Widely regarded as one of the great Arab poets of the modern period, he currently lives in temporary exile in Uxbridge, a London suburb close to Heathrow Airport and a long way from the village of Abulkhasib, near Basrah, where he was born in 1934, and from Baghdad where he spent his formative years. I smiled when he told me he lived near the airport. It reminded me of a Brecht poem on exile, migration and asylum:

---

6 *Without An Alphabet, Without a Face: Selected Poems of Saadi Youssef*, translated by Khaled Mattawa, St Paul, 2002.

I always found the name false which they gave us: Emigrants.

That means those who leave their country. But we

Did not leave, of our own free will,

Choosing another land. Nor did we enter

Into a land, to stay there, if possible for ever.

Merely, we fled. We are driven out, banned.

Not a home, but an exile, shall the land be that took us in.

Restlessly we wait thus, as near as we can to the frontier. […][7]

The next day we met in the Soho offices of the *New Left Review*.

'Where would you like to eat?'

'Oh,' and then with a nonchalant shrug, 'anywhere.'

As we walked through the streets inspecting one local eatery after another, my offers of Chinese, Vietnamese, Japanese, and Thai restaurants were systematically rejected.

'Let's not eat Far Eastern.'

After another futile search for something else I suggested he should decide on the cuisine.

'Is there an Arab café or something?'

There was one on Greek Street. It was empty and that's where we ended up having lunch. He recognised the Algerian accent of the waiter. The music was loud and we asked them to turn it down.

'That was a Nizar Qabbani poem being sung,' he told me. 'You like his work, don't you?'

I did, but it was still too loud. We talked of Qabbani for a while and of the Pakistani poet Faiz, whom Youssef had met in Beirut a quarter of a century ago, when both were in exile. He liked Faiz and asked about his

---

7 Bertolt Brecht, 'Concerning the Label Emigrant', in *Poems 1913–1956*, edited by John Willet and Ralph Manheim, London, 1976, p. 301.

impact on Pakistani culture. 'For many of us growing up under a dictatorship,' I told him, 'Faiz was Pakistani culture.' Qabbani and Faiz were both dead but the poetry lived and it would last. He talked of poets he had translated into Arabic: Whitman, Cavafy, Ritsos, Ungaretti, and Lorca. When I asked about his own work and reputation, he insisted that he was not alone. Iraq had been blessed with poets.

'There were three of us from an older generation: al-Jawahiri, Mudhaffar al-Nawab, and myself. All of us ended up in exile. I think al-Jawahiri was a hundred years old when he died a few years ago [in 1997] in Damascus. Never saw Baghdad again. Saddam was always sending his emissaries to plead with us. He wanted all three of us to return for a public poetry reading in Baghdad. He knew and we knew that if this happened there would be at least half a million people at the event, if not more. Through his messenger he told us "I know you're all communists and you attack me, but understand that you're also part of our national heritage. Please return. The blood on my neck will guarantee your safety." Somehow this was not a very reassuring message. In any case too many of our friends and comrades had been tortured and killed. That's the deal he made with the Americans at the time. He would wipe us out and not just us. There were some very committed and decent people in the Ba'ath Party as well. They, too, perished. So we did not return to Baghdad. And now it's occupied again.'

Exile had not tamed these poets. Their poetry circulated inside a country where their acidic verses were much appreciated. Their experience of the regime and its Western backers had not made them embittered and disillusioned old renegades, speaking in a servile and self-deprecating idiom as they queued for Saudi largesse. In his yearning for home, Mudhaffar al-Nawab had spoken for a whole generation of exiles:

> I have accepted my fate
> Is like that of a bird,

And I have endured all
Except humiliation,
Or having my heart
Caged in the Sultan's palace.
But dear God
Even birds have homes to return to,
I fly across this homeland
From sea to sea,
And to prison after prison after prison,
Each jailer embracing the other.[8]

Saadi Youssef paused as he lit another cigarette. We were both depressed. He had not seen his two sisters, who lived in Basrah, since 1978. Were they still there? The memory and history of the people was being looted. The Baghdad Museum contained antiquities that dated back to early Mesopotamian civilisation (writing was invented there in 3500BC). Thieves and some GIs (according to photographs circulated on the Internet) had ransacked the building after a tank shell had destroyed the front door; the Baghdad Library had been set alight yet again, under the watchful eyes of the occupying soldiers, and priceless documents of the Ottoman period lay scattered and burnt on the pavements outside. The ziggurat on the ancient site of the royal city of Ur had been graffitied by triumphant US soldiers. Further south, a unit of British soldiers were photographing themselves torturing and sexually assaulting Iraqi

---

8 Translated by Wadood Hammad. The poem narrates its author's experiences in the early sixties. Mudhaffar was imprisoned after the first Ba'athist coup of 1963 (see Chapter 3) and tortured. Together with other prisoners, he managed to escape from prison; they crossed the Iranian border to Ahwaz in Khuzestan, an ethnic Arab province. His presence was soon discovered by SAVAK, the Shah's secret police. They were arrested, tortured, and returned to Baghdad.

men and women. It was the unchanging face of history. Military occupation, economic exploitation, sexual and cultural humiliation had been the time-honoured methods of empires old and new. How else could a country be recolonised against its will? In 1919 the British had opted for an Arab façade, but with total British control of everything else. It had ended badly. An exact repeat would be difficult, but the choices were limited.

As a born-again Christian fundamentalist, Bush obviously was aware of the wickedness of ancient Babylon (an Old Testament favourite) and the associated rhymes. Possibly he was also aware that its ruins were located in Mesopotamia, which was now Iraq, but did he know much else? Had anyone enlightened him on Baghdad and its history? Did he know why the US occupiers were being referred to as the 'new Mongols'? Did any of them know what had happened in the thirteenth century when Hulegu Khan's warriors had laid siege to the city? The Mongols were a people without a written culture and always felt threatened by books, manuscripts, and libraries. When Hulegu's warriors burnt the Baghdad Library in 1258 they were destroying something which they foolishly thought could be used against them. This act of barbarism led to the destruction of thousands of valued manuscripts including rare translations of ancient Greek texts. Whether some of the plays of Aristophanes were lost for ever in this fire or in that which destroyed the library in Alexandria remains a subject for debate. What is undisputed is the loss suffered by Islamic and world culture. Memories may be stored in the vaults of a museum situated in one city, but they belong to the world. The burning of books in Baghdad by the Mongols and by the Catholics in Granada two hundred years later are unforgotten episodes in the Islamic world.

The American generals in command of the army occupying Baghdad in 2003 had a responsibility to safeguard its cultural treasures. They failed abysmally. Having stirred their soldiers to fight and destroy the 'rag-heads', portrayed in briefings as uncivilised barbarians responsible for 9/11, perhaps they were now fearful of admitting that the 'ragheads' were a people with a culture. Whatever the reason, nothing was done.

Every few minutes Saadi Youssef would shake his head in despair and disbelief: 'Who would have thought the West would be back again.' And then he expressed an unshaken confidence in his people. 'We have a long history of resistance. Did you know that al-Jawahiri's brother was badly wounded during the 1948 uprising against the British? He died in al-Jawahiri's arms, not far from the Jisr al-Shuhada [The Bridge of Martyrs] on the Tigris where the bullets had felled him. How could the blood stains be erased? This occupation will not be accepted for too long. Nor will their puppets.'

Al-Jawahiri had commemorated the 1948 anti-British uprising with a poem whose opening lines were recalled by many Iraqis the week that Baghdad fell:

> I see a horizon lit with blood,
> And many a starless night.
> A generation comes and another goes
> And the fire keeps burning.

One of those who evoked the poem from his Cairene exile was Sinan Antoon, an Iraqi poet of a younger generation, who informed the readers of *al-Ahram* how

> the last few years of the Iraq–Iran war (1980–1988) haunted our youth and brought nihilism to our lives. During this period, the dark and dreary bars on Abu-Nuwwas Street were our haven, and we remained true to the poet's spirit and his wine songs expressing disillusionment

with the here and now, but also gaiety, light-heartedness and hedonism to combat its ephemera. The dissident contemporary Iraqi poet Mudhaffar al-Nawab was our guide on our way back home at night. His fiery, banned poems were smuggled into Iraq on cassettes and circulated secretly among friends. Some of those friends stayed in Iraq, withering under the sanctions and now another war, while many ended up in various types of exile.

And now the Arab nation had suffered yet another defeat. An independent sovereign Arab state had been invaded and occupied and this, especially because of the lack of resistance in Baghdad, brought back memories of other defeats. After Baghdad had fallen in 1258 a conversation took place in the palace between the Mongol leader Hulegu Khan and al-Mustasim, the Commander of the Faithful and last of the Abbasid Caliphs. The major historians of that time explain the defeat of the Caliph in terms of a lack of preparation and bitter factional struggles between Shia and Sunni notables. Some allege that the Governor of Mosul and the Wazir al-Alqami (senior Minister of the Court), a Shia, literally sold out to the Mongols and betrayed their ruler. The historian al-Athir charges the Wazir with having advised the Caliph to reduce the size of the army so that only 10,000 soldiers were left to defend the city against a Mongol cavalry of 200,000 men. Others still point the finger at the Kurds who had backed a previous Mongol expedition.

It is a fact that Baghdad was riven by intra-Muslim factionalism, linked to networks of patronage and power. Whether the Caliph was betrayed by Shia, Kurds or himself is still disputed. What is generally agreed, however, by Arab and non-Arab sources is the account given by the philosopher Nasir al-Din al-Tusi (d.1274), who was present during the celebrated conversation between the Mongol conqueror and the defeated Caliph. Here, it has to be said, the political acumen displayed by the 'barbarian'

Hulegu was infinitely superior to that of his fallen rival, who had the advantage of being surrounded by some of the most refined scholars in the world. According to al-Tusi:

> The King [Hulegu] went to examine the Caliph's residence and walked about it in every direction. The Caliph was fetched and ordered presents to be offered. Whatever he brought out the King at once distributed amongst his suite and emirs, as well as among military leaders and all those present. He then set a golden tray before the Caliph and said: 'Eat!'
>
> 'It is not edible,' said the Caliph.
>
> 'Then why didst thou keep it,' asked the King, 'and not give it to thy soldiers? And why didst thou not make these iron doors into arrow-heads and come to the banks of the river so that I might not have been able to cross it?'
>
> 'Such,' replied the Caliph, 'was God's will.'
>
> 'What will befall thee,' said the King, 'is also God's will.'

Baghdad never recovered from that defeat. The Mongols had no desire to stay in the city. They looted and killed, but they left, taking with them a great deal of treasure and many women. Henceforth Tabriz in Persia became the centre of trade and Hormuz replaced Basrah as the principal port of trade in the region. From 1258 onwards Baghdad became a provincial city with a declining population, plagued by floods and other disasters and ruled by Mongols, Persians, the Ottomans, and subsequently the British (who instituted a monarchy). Freedom from foreign rule for the region came seven centuries later, in 1958 – the high point of Arab nationalism – and in virtually every instance it was the army that became the repository of nationalism. How had this come about?

In 1948 the weak and divided Arab armies (mostly controlled by the British) were hurled into battle with Israel. Defeat was not inevitable, but

Abderrahman Munif.

Intishal Al-Timimi

the political and military leaders of the Arab states, in polar contrast to the Zionist leadership, lacked the will to win. The Zionists, armed by the retreating British Empire, had organised and trained their supporters well. The Arabs were disabled and disarmed by the corrupt elite that led them.

In his memoirs, the Saudi novelist Abderrahman Munif wrote of his childhood and youth in Amman. His mother was an Iraqi and his grandmother would often return from Baghdad bearing strange new headgear and lots of stories. Munif heard how the leaders of the anti-British rebellion in 1941 had been captured by Sir John Glubb, brought back to Baghdad and hanged. Glubb lived in Amman and here, too, his legionnaires wreaked havoc. Pro-Palestinian demonstrations in 1947–48 were brutally repressed, but the sympathy for the victims on the other side of the River Jordan could never be crushed. Munif describes the atmosphere in school:

> Sometimes, the names of the cities in other Arab countries were confused with one another or not easily remembered, but all the hands of the students would shoot up when the teacher asked who could name five cities in Palestine. Voices competed drowning each other out: Jerusalem, Jaffa, Haifa, Gaza, Lydda, Ramlah, Acre, Safad, Ramallah, Hebron… Palestine was more than just a land and a people. In the mind of every

Arab it is a constellation of meanings, symbols and connotations which have accumulated and filtered down through several generations.[9]

As the first detachment of Iraqi soldiers began to arrive in Amman, supposedly on their way to Palestine, they were welcomed by an over-joyed people, including Munif's grandmother, who recognised a distant relation, Ismail, amongst the soldiery. The Iraqis were fed and housed free of charge and 'the people of the city sprinkled rice, wheat and flowers on the soldiers when they marched past'. But the rest of the force did not arrive. Their officers delayed troop movements till it was too late. Hope turned to anxiety and then anger. Ismail was shattered by the betrayal.

'Pimps!' he shouted. 'What morals! Where were your maps, where were your plans, what were you going to do? They left us in the open and said, "orders will reach you." And we knew nothing. Should we have been on the offensive or the defensive? Should we have hidden in trenches and protected ourselves, or should we have just carried away our stuff and left?'

Grandmother tried to comfort him. 'Ismail, don't get upset. There's always a lot of messing about and everything takes time to work out.'

'You mean after we have died like dogs?'

'God forbid…'

'So where are they, those rascals whose chests are decked out with medals? They said they would liberate Palestine in two days.'

The same thing happened to a thousand Ismails along all the fronts. Between 15 May and 21 June [1948], when the first armistice was declared, cities fell, thousands were killed and hundreds of thousands made homeless.

---

9 *Story of a City: A Childhood in Amman*, by Abderrahman Munif, London, 1996.

This defeat led to a process of rapid radicalisation throughout the Arab world. The people did not need to be told why the Arab armies had failed to prevent the catastrophe. They knew that the Generals were dominated by the British and destined only to be the pallbearers in the funeral cortege of Palestine. Nor was this view confined to the bazaar. In the heart of each Arab army there were groups of young nationalist-minded officers who felt deeply humiliated and began to organise in secret. They were determined to change for ever the ritual formulae of subservience to imperial interests that had led to the catastrophe. The military revolutions of the fifties that toppled the pro-British monarchies in Egypt and Iraq were a direct outcome of the 1948 defeat.

In 2003, a week before they began to bomb Baghdad, purely by chance I ran into a group of Arab friends near Westminster Bridge, not far from the Mother of Parliaments that would soon approve yet another imperial war. Meeting them was a real relief, something they could not have realised. I had come straight out from participating in a slightly claustrophobic BBC television debate on Iraq. As a giant image of Richard Perle smiled cynically from a Washington studio, the British Foreign Secretary (a weasel of many years' standing) had insisted that the only purpose of invading Iraq was disarmament and not regime change. In another corner, two Peninsular potentates from the Hashemite and al-Saud dynasties exchanged mild insults.[10] A few of us had managed to get in a few words challenging the Anglo-American establishment consensus.

---

10   While Prince Hassan of Jordan insisted that Islam was not incompatible with democracy, Prince Turki bin Faisal, the Saudi Ambassador in Britain and former head of intelligence, stated the opposite and reminded the audience that Osama had played a glorious role in fighting the Russians in Afghanistan with the complete approval of the West. Later, Hassan told me of a recent experience he had had in Scotland. At a public lecture, a local notable had, after a long preamble, asked the audience to join him in welcoming a prince from the oldest Arab family and with the most distinguished lineage, 'Prince Hassan bin Laden.' As we laughed, Hassan said: 'It seems we're back to square one, Tariq. They can't tell one Arab from another.'

After all this, encountering a few street Arabs was pure ozone. We talked of the coming war, its likely impact, whether or not there would be a resistance, and so on. I was undecided whether to accept an invitation to dinner till the friend inviting me home said: 'We've just bought two videos with old footage of Nasser.' I was now happy to be dragged back to watch Nasser in Knightsbridge. It was an eerie and moving experience. Eerie because of the timing. Nearly half a century after the Suez war, another Arab country was preparing to be invaded by two imperialist powers backed by Israel. This time the United States had replaced France. Moving because the documentary films concentrated on Nasser's rapport with the Arab street, his 1956 defiance of the aging British lion ('Let the imperialists choke in their rage') as he announced the nationalisation of the Suez Canal – there were scenes of a population wild with delight. Here was an Arab leader who, despite all his weaknesses, was genuinely popular with his people, unlike the freaks and monsters that came later. The depiction of the mass mobilisations throughout the Arab world was stunning. The refusal by the people to accept Nasser's resignation after the 1967 defeat, the genuine displays of grief at his funeral as people instinctively realised that an important period of their history had come to an end. Not much was said after the films ended. What was there to say? And yet all of us were thinking how much the world had changed. In 1956 when Britain, France and Israel invaded Egypt, it was seen as a pre-emptive assault on the entire Arab nation. The Suez Canal was blocked; oil pipelines and pumping stations in Iraq and Syria were blown up; the Saudis refused to pump any oil that might be loaded on to French or British tankers and the flow from Saudi oilfields to Bahrain came to a total halt. Explosives were even planted underneath the oil installations in Kuwait, then and now, little more than an imperial petrol station. And this time? Would the Arab states do anything remotely similar to punish the invader of Iraq? It seemed unrealistic even to pose such a question.

The second pre-emptive strike, this time from Israel alone, came in 1967. It took the Egyptian nationalists by surprise and was a body blow against Arab nationalism, which never recovered. A decade after Gamal Abdel Nasser's death his successor, Anwar Saadat, had sold himself and the state to the American Empire. It was to be neo-liberalism at home and the recognition of Israel. Saadat paid the price with his own blood. Islamist soldiers had managed to substitute real bullets for the blanks and executed him in public view during a ceremonial parade. This made every dictator nervous. Soldiers are now carefully watched before and during these events.

Another pre-emptive strike, this time a direct one, has led to the occupation of Iraq. The plan was to install a market-fundamentalist regime and recognise Israel within 'three months', but the process has been delayed by the refusal of most Iraqis to collaborate. Whatever happens in Iraq over the next five years, the consequences of this occupation will mark this century. In 1928, under British occupation, the Iraqi poet Jamil Sidqi az-Zahawi, angered by the passivity of some of his countrymen, especially the fatalists drenched in obscurantism, asked Iraqis to challenge everything that prevented resistance: 'Rise in violent anger against old usages/ Rise even against Providence'.

Today, his poetic heirs, Saadi Youssef and Mudhaffar al-Nawab, look at their country from afar and think. What are they thinking? On the eve of the 2003 war, while Anglo-American politicians and their favoured journalists were busy stifling dissent with a barrage of lies, a platoon of carefully chosen quislings were assembled in a London hotel to discuss the future of Iraq after 'liberation'. It conjured an image in the poet's mind of a 'jackals' wedding'. In southern Iraq, on a summer's night, in order to recover from the day's heat, people in the villages often sleep in the open air, underneath a starlit sky. Their peace is sometimes disturbed by a conclave of noisy jackals, some engaged in mating, others clamouring to be next, and a few simply quarrelling. After an hour or more it reaches a climax. By this time the noise and stench is unbearable. Suddenly, the animals depart. Next time they will meet elsewhere, but wherever and whenever they do, the villagers recall, with disgust, the nights disturbed by a 'jackals' wedding'.

Saadi Youssef composed a new poem, addressed it to his exiled fellow poet in Damascus and titled it 'The Jackals' Wedding':[11]

> O Mudhaffar al-Nawab,
>
> my life-long comrade,
>
> what are we to do about the jackals' wedding?
>
> You remember the old days:
>
> In the cool of the evening
>
> under a bamboo roof
>
> propped on soft cushions stuffed with fine wool
>
> we'd sip tea (a tea I've never since tasted)
>
> among friends …
>
> Night falls as softly as our words
>
> under the darkening crowns of the date palms
>
> while smoke curls from the hearth, such fragrance
>
> as if the universe had just begun
>
> …
>
> Then a cackling explodes
>
> from the long grass and date palms –
>
> the jackals' wedding!
>
> …

---

11 Translated for this book by Saadi Youssef, Hafiz Kheir, and Sarah Maguire, for which I am enormously grateful. The poem had the desired effect: the pro-occupation gathering is now referred to as 'the jackals' wedding' by many Iraqis.

O, Mudhaffar al-Nawab –
today isn't yesterday
(truth is as evanescent as the dream of a child) –
truth is, this time we're at their wedding reception,
yes, the jackals' wedding
you've read their invitation:

For tho' we trudge past Dahna[12] empty-handed
We depart Dareen[13] our purses lined with gold.
'While the townsfolk attend to their affairs
Now, Zuraik,[14] fleece them, quick as a fox!'
…

O, Mudhaffar al-Nawab,
let's make a deal:

I'll go in your place
(Damascus is too far away from that secret hotel …)
I'll spit in the jackals' faces,
I'll spit on their lists,
I'll declare that we are the people of Iraq –
we are the ancestral trees of this land,
proud beneath our modest roof of bamboo.

The cyberspace revolution ensured that the poem reached Baghdad and Basrah within minutes of being completed and from there it travelled everywhere in Iraq. And many who read it nodded their heads in amusement. They understood the poet just as he understood them.

12,13,14   These are all references to pre-Islamic texts, often used in Arabic grammar textbooks.

(AP Photo/Marwan Naamani, Pool)

The jackals' wedding: members of Iraq's so-called Governing Council, central Baghdad, 13 July 2003.

The jackals, incapable of competing with the poem, began to hurl hate-filled darts at the poet. Their venom was spat out in public. Saadi Youssef began to be denounced regularly in the *Daily Jackal* and the *Liberated Jackal News* and the rest of the jackal press produced by those who wanted to impose themselves on Iraq not by appealing to those who live there but by standing on the shoulders of the occupying armies and shouting that they were the rightful rulers. A few cursed jackals even began to harass the poet at home: threatening e-mails and anonymous

Mudhaffar al-Nawab.

phone calls were received every day. His life-comrade in Damascus also began to be vilified.

A jackal alleged that Mudhaffar al-Nawab was not a real Iraqi because his family originally came from Kashmir in India. Let us not bother to ask from where they first went to India. Let us not even speak of the prison sentences and tortures suffered by this poet for his beliefs. He fought like a tiger before they captured him. The notion that only 'real' Iraqis, i.e., jackals, can speak for Iraq today comes strangely from those celebrating a new imperial occupation. But the rage felt by the jackals was revealing. Could anyone have asked for a better demonstration of the power still enjoyed by poetry in the Arab world? From Damascus in March 2003, Mudhaffar al-Nawab observed the war preparations and the plans to recolonise his country and penned a sober warning:[15]

> Would you ever forgive a lynch mob
> Because they pulled your stiff corpse
> From the gallows?

---

15 Translated for this book by Sarah Maguire and Hafiz Kheiri.

And never trust a freedom fighter
Who turns up with no arms –
Believe me, I got burnt in that crematorium.

Truth is, you're only as big as your cannons,
While the crowds who wave knives and forks
Simply have eyes for their stomachs.
O my people in love with our homeland,
I'm not scared of barbarians gathered at our gates.
No, I'm afraid of the enemies within –

Tyranny, Autocracy, Dictatorship.

An Early Letter to General Tommy Franks
Saadi Youssef (Poet from Mesopotamia)

Sir, General

First, I want to say, in all honesty, that I am following what is permitted
on the TV about your news: about your close ranked soldiers, with your
family, with your president, etc … And that when I observe History – in
a differential way – I feel that I would like to be like one of my ancestors
who saved a city from being razed by Tamerlane in Syria.

You will enter, Sir, General, Baghdad, like all who entered, before you:
a conqueror …

But you know, due to the fact that you were a conquered nation once,
that nations are unconquerable.

Rulers can be defeated. And our ruler will be defeated first. I am
happy about that, because this imbecile denied me the air of my country
for more than thirty years.

You do not like Julius Caesar: you say, he was a general, but with long speeches, so he was killed!

I, the poet, will be short instead.

You will enter Baghdad, Sir, General; can I relay to you what Omar (the second Caliph after Mohammed) advised his general who was heading for Iraq?

Don't cut down a single tree, he said.

But today things are taking a different turn; it is said that you want to cut the return route of Iraqis going back to their country. Rumour has it that a list of 2,000 Iraqi opponents, prepared by your Iraqi agents, prohibits these Iraqis going back to their homeland, under the pretext of easing your occupation.

In so far as this concerns me, I can't deny this rumour in a soft way.

Al-Mutamar (an Arabic weekly, financed by the American taxpayer, and based in London) has recently published a letter saying that I the poet, Saadi Youssef, must be denied the right of return to Iraq, after its ('liberation').

I am asking you

And Jonny Abu-Zaid, our in-coming Governor General

To elaborate on Human Rights under conditions of imminent occupation.

London, 1 March 2003
(written in English after learning that his name was on a list of undesirables)

Meanwhile, another jackals' wedding took place in occupied Baghdad in July 2003. A US-appointed 'Governing Council of Iraq' consisting of jackals of every stripe was presented to the assembled media. The presence of the Iraqi Communist Party was no surprise. Its leaders had been ensconced in discussions with Bremer since the occupation. Unlike its

Eastern European counterparts, the party had not changed its name, but its politics, to the extent that they exist, are no different from those of the former Communist Parties of Poland or Bulgaria, a fact reflected in graffiti on a Baghdad wall: ICP = Iraqi Collaborators Party.

The presence on the 'Governing Council' of veteran Iraqi politician Adnan Pachachi, however, represented a political somersault. Just prior to the war, Pachachi had declared publicly in the *Financial Times* of 3 March 2003 that Iraqi nationalism was still a vibrant force and:

> This is the reason I have rejected offers to take a leading part in the arrangements for the post-Saddam era … I declined for three reasons. First, I have serious doubts about the legitimacy of such a group or its representative nature. Second, any body formed by such a group would have only advisory responsibilities during the transitional period, not executive ones. Serving as an advisory body attached to a US military administration would be damaging and unacceptable. Third, I have reservations about the group's structure and membership …

All these doubts vanished four months later, but the objections remain valid. The 'Governing Council' is an unstable structure and could be ripped apart if the resistance continues to increase, forcing some of its members to think again. The aim of the Iraqi *maquis* is to target the occupation forces on a daily basis. In this they appear to have been successful. And the replacement of US soldiers by UN mercenaries is unlikely to improve the situation. Ultimately the jackals and their masters will fail.

3

An Oligarchy of Racketeers

The self-definition of the British Empire was summarised accurately in a sentence published in a report that established the Committee of Imperial Defence in 1904: 'The British Empire is pre-eminently a great Naval, Indian and Colonial power.'[16] This emphasis on India was not misplaced. The men and materials provided by the subcontinent were a crucial pillar of global colonial hegemony. Post-slavery, poor Indian peasants were encouraged to uproot themselves, cross the ocean and work the plantations of Trinidad and Guyana; clerks were despatched to help administer East and South Africa; Sikhs and Gurkhas were used to crush the Boxer rebellion in China and turbulence elsewhere. Later, Indian troops were used to good effect in both world wars as well as in the colonisation of the Arab world during the inter-war period. The establishment of imperial beachheads in those days required gunboats (naval supremacy) plus Gurkhas.

---

16   Quoted in *Britain's Moment in the Middle East: 1914–1956,* by Elizabeth Monroe, London, 1963. This was one of the prescribed course books I had to read for the study of International Relations at Oxford. At the time it enraged me as a classic liberal defence of Empire. Re-reading it forty years later elicits the same reaction, but in the current post-post-colonial period I read it calmly, viewing it as an aid to understanding the continuities, discontinuities, and contrasts between the imperialism that is currently on offer and that of the past.

In 1917 the British, with the help of colonial soldiers from India, took Jerusalem and Baghdad. Thus ended a long period of Ottoman rule that had defined and moulded the region for many centuries. It had permitted many of the regions to enjoy virtual autonomy as long as the taxes were paid regularly into the imperial treasury in Istanbul. Because of its age, the Ottoman Empire was far more relaxed than its modern European rivals and tormentors. Would it have made any difference if the Ottoman Empire had remained neutral during the First World War? Perhaps not, but if Istanbul had fought actively alongside London and Paris, like the Japanese, the post-war picture would certainly have been far more complex. The borders of the states that would have emerged might have been very different and as for the Balfour Declaration, its implementation might not have been as simple had the British army not been present in the region.

The Ottoman domination of the Arab world began in the sixteenth century and was completed by the victory of the Turkish artillery and muskets over the badly equipped and poorly led army of the Mamluk Sultan of Egypt, following which the holy cities of Mecca and Medina became part of the Empire just like Damascus, Baghdad, Tripoli, and Algiers. The preachers were the first to change sides and record their loyalty to the new order. The week after the city fell, the Friday prayers in all of Cairo's mosques began thus:

O Lord! Uphold the Sultan, son of the sultan, ruler over both lands and the two seas, conqueror of both hosts, monarch of the two Iraqs, minister of the two Holy Cities, the victorious Sultan Selim Shah. Grant him, O Lord, thy precious aid; enable him to win glorious victories.

Ottoman rule was accepted for a number of reasons. It was a Muslim Empire with a Caliph at its head and the Caliph was now recognised as such throughout the house of Islam, with the exception of Shiite Persia. For the majority of Muslims this marked the first extended period in their history when there was a single centre of temporal and spiritual authority. Islam had penetrated the Anatolian tribes soon after its emergence. As the Romans had learnt from the Greeks, so too had the Turkish rulers imbibed Arab learning, culture, and traditions: science, religion, and the alphabet. While these were the foundation stones of the new Empire, the house built above them was a synthesis: Persian art, poetry and absolute monarchism; Byzantine methods of military and civil administration; and a nomadic generosity that encouraged assimilation. The combination proved fertile in the fields of statecraft, architecture, and literature.

All this – Ottomanism – became the common heritage of the people who lived in cities and districts throughout the Arab world. The Caliph-Sultan did not insist on total control or obedience so long as the taxes were paid into the Treasury at Istanbul. As a result, the more gifted Governors enjoyed a relative autonomy, which discouraged them from attempting a total break. Baghdad, Basrah and Mosul had to be retaken by an Ottoman army in 1831 when the appointed Governor refused to make way for a successor. In the decades that followed, administrative and land reforms were instituted, which abandoned the centuries-old pattern of state ownership in favour of individual proprietors. This created a new class of landlord-sheikhs (usually heads of tribes and clans) and a new base of social power, which would be deployed by the British a century later to maintain control. Politically, the emergence of reformist currents within the Ottoman Empire, the convening of a parliament in Istanbul as well as the 1906 Constitutional Revolution in Persia began to excite Arab hopes as well. Arabs were represented in the Ottoman parliament, but increasingly they began to demand that Arabic be given equal status with Turkish and raised the issue of local participatory assemblies. In preceding centuries, Ottoman laxity might well have tolerated all this, but the reformist regime in Istanbul was imbued with a strong Turkish nationalism and it became fearful that its own example might lead to a detachment of its empire. This led it away from decentralisation. Its disappointed subjects began to organise clandestinely. It was Arab officers in the Ottoman army who first organised secret societies in Baghdad and Basrah. Here, too, they were merely following an earlier pattern established by those who were now in power in Istanbul.

Towards the end of the nineteenth century, the rival British Empire encouraged the emergence of anti-Ottoman currents in the Arab East. Some of this new opposition was nationalist, but most of the tribal chiefs were basically opportunist. Inter-imperial rivalry led to the targeting of particular families and tribes, who were only too willing to switch sides in return for cash and arms. Lord Kitchener had served in Palestine and Egypt. He had already established an early contact with the Hashemite family, the hereditary guardians of Mecca and Medina, but had remained non-committal for fear of damaging Anglo-Turkish relations. A month after the outbreak of the First World War, in his capacity as Minister for War, Kitchener sent a celebrated handwritten letter to the Sharif of Mecca and his son Abdullah. He wondered where the Arabs would stand if the Kaiser dragged Turkey into the war. With characteristic imperial mendacity he then made the following offer:

Till now we have defended and befriended Islam in the person of the Turks. Henceforth it shall be that of the noble Arab. It may be that an Arab of true race will assume the Khalifate at Mecca or Medina, and so good may come by the help of God out of all the evil, which is now occurring. It would be well if your Highness could convey to your followers and devotees who are found throughout the world in every country the good tidings of the freedom of the Arabs and the rising of the sun over Arabia.[17]

Kitchener himself did not live to savour his triumph. The Deep claimed him. But the victories and defeats of the First World War became the bridge for the departure of one empire and the entry of another. As Ottoman soldiers trundled westwards, their British and French replacements marched eastwards. The Anglo-French (Sykes–Picot) agreement to share the spoils of war led to the division of the Arab East and the creation of new states and new frontiers that provided a real impetus to the embryonic nationalist currents already in existence. The Hashemite and al-Saud clans were built up by the British as a protective dam against both nationalism and 'the syndicalist and socialistic ideas seeping out of Europe', in the words of Gertrude Bell.[18]

Bell mapped the frontiers of the new state of Iraq: the three Ottoman provinces of Baghdad, Basrah, and Mosul were crudely stitched together. Mosul had been detached from Turkey in blatant violation of the agreed armistice terms. Curzon had brushed aside Turkish protests with choice insults, the prerogative of the victor, but this did not resolve the inter-departmental dispute which now erupted regarding the management of the new state. In Egypt, the British had opted for 'maintenance of the King's Protectorate' to preserve their monopoly of the Suez Canal, vital for the link with India. The Mesopotamian quandary persisted. The League

---

17 Monroe, op cit, p. 27.
18 Gertrude Bell was an extremely intelligent administrator of the Empire. In an astute recent appraisal ('Miss Bell's Lines in the Sand', *Guardian*, 12 March 2003), James Buchan writes: 'Her letters to her father and stepmother, one of the great correspondences of the past century, pass easily from orders for cotton gowns at Harvey and Nichols [sic] to the new-fangled British air warfare being tried out on recalcitrant Iraqi Arabs and Kurds.' This was the first time that chemical weapons (in the shape of mustard gas) were used in the region.

of Nations Mandate had not specified how Britain should administer the state. The British Indian government wanted the new state to be run just like India and preferably under the tutelage of Delhi. To their surprise, Curzon, who presided over the committee making the decisions, vetoed the project, opting instead for Gertrude Bell's plan of total British control behind an Arab smokescreen. This was regarded as a more subtle form of domination. It was also more convenient. The Mesopotamian Expeditionary Force that had seized the three Ottoman provinces was composed of Indian sepoys. The growing turmoil in India necessitated their early return to help maintain imperial order at home. If carefully nurtured and protected, Arab dynasties could in due course become the trusted custodians of the new imperial possessions.

As the Ottoman Empire began to disintegrate, the secret societies in Mesopotamia became more public and split. The opportunists amongst them were eager to ingratiate themselves with Caliph Curzon, and being good opportunists they understood that those who changed sides first would receive the greatest rewards. One such person was Nuri al-Said, a former officer in the Ottoman army. But others, including local notables, tribal chiefs and religious leaders were more circumspect. They felt that the new Empire might be much worse than the defeated Ottomans and here they were not so wrong.

History appeared to be on the side of Nuri al-Said and the family of Sharif Hussein of Mecca, who had accepted Kitchener's offer and collaborated happily with T.E. Lawrence and General Allenby. In return he was promised the kingdom of the Hijaz in the Peninsula and his son Feisal was seduced by the offer of a greater Syria. The white men spoke with forked tongues. H.S. Philby had already promised the Peninsula to the al-Saud family, which Britain had been funding and arming for many years. In 1924 their leader, Ibn Saud, became impatient. Completely unprovoked, he attacked and defeated Sharif Hussein. The Hashemite chief was forced to abandon the guardianship of the Holy Cities and compelled to leave the Hijaz. He died in exile in 1931. The rivalry between the two clans has not abated to this day.

Two of Sharif Hussein's sons were later provided with kingdoms, but not the realms they had coveted. In 1919, Feisal had reached Damascus with his Bedouin cavalry, but the following year he was unceremoniously removed by French troops. The French preferred to impose their own model on their colonial possessions and this did not include a monarchy. Now Feisal was without a throne. Enter Gertrude Bell stage right. Both she and her boss, Sir Percy Cox, felt that the new country they had created required a king. Lengthy inter-departmental negotiations finally resulted in approval for the project. The Hashemites had been completely loyal, they felt hurt and a soothing balm was required. Abdullah was made King of Jordan and Bell intrigued non-stop to place Emir Feisal on the newly created throne of Iraq, with Jafar Askari as a leading *consigliore* and the most trusted imperial agent in the new royal entourage. In a world filled with unreliables, men like Askari were rare. 'I'll never engage in creating kings again; it's too great a strain,' Gertrude Bell would later complain with more than a touch of imperial vanity, even though the actual decision was made in 1921 by the Colonial Secretary, Winston Churchill, who had convened a conference in Cairo to settle all petty disputes.

Iraqis who felt that Feisal had been foisted on them, however, were the ones who really suffered. The Kurds, who had initially welcomed the British, became disaffected as they were denied any real autonomy: they had already given a practical demonstration of their alienation in 1919–20 by launching an anti-British rebellion in Sulaymaniyah. Their leader, Mahmud Barzinji, was captured and received the death sentence, which was later commuted to exile in Kuwait (which for some Kurds was the equivalent of hell in any case). This showed foresight as the British would need him again in 1922. The Kurds had been crushed by the combined use of both ground troops and air power. The Arab leaders did not raise the flag of revolt, but one of their leaders, Sayyid Talib al-Naqib, made no secret of his anger and denounced Feisal as an interloper. The British deported him from the country. But the popular mood in the south was equally antagonistic. In June 1920 the arrest of a local leader in Rumaitha for refusing to pay taxes to the British authorities sparked off a new revolt. An armed group raided the prison, released their leader and then proceeded to destroy bridges and railway lines to delay reinforcements. Within days the rebellion spread to Samawa (where the British officers surrendered) and then to the Shia stronghold of Najaf. The British Governor did not wait to be despatched. At the first sign of unrest he wisely left the city. The whole of the lower Euphrates region was now infected by a rebellion that would last for over six months and cost the imperial army the lives of 2,000 soldiers. Iraqi casualties were four times as high. The ideological patter deployed by imperial occupiers has not changed much over the last 100 or more years. In 1914, a few years prior to the Euphrates uprising, Bell's boss Sir Percy Cox had informed the citizens of Basrah that the British came as 'liberators, not conquerors'. Few were deceived and there was overwhelming popular support for the *fatwas* which called for a holy war against the infidel occupation.

A majority of the traditional Sunni leaders, who had worked closely with the Ottomans, was also annoyed at being bypassed, and Emir Feisal came to a country where he had little real support from either the elite or the population at large. Sunni–Shia unity was boosted by a desire to fight the common enemy and by secret societies such as Haras al-Istiqlal, which pushed strongly for unity against the British. Throughout the 1920s, the appeals of the poet Muhammad al-Obeidi were heard in the cities on the Tigris and the mid-Euphrates:

Set fire noble Iraqis
wash our shame with blood
We are not slaves
to adorn our necks with collars
We are not prisoners
to submit ourselves to be manacled
We are not women
whose only weapon is the tear
We are not orphans
that seek a Mandate for Iraq
And if we bow before oppression
We shall forfeit the pleasures of the Tigris

Given this mood, which was widespread, Feisal became increasingly dependent on the British and the tiny clique of former Ottoman officers who had joined him in 1916. Nuri al-Said was appointed Chief of Staff of the tiny Iraqi army by his brother-in-law Jafar Askari, a key operator in the royal entourage. Meanwhile the Arab population as a whole found itself locked in by new structures of domination. The half-hearted land-lordism of the late-Ottoman period was transformed into a hard-hearted arrangement: the proprietors were showered with privilege and used to police the new order. Class solidarity was utilised, as in India, to defuse nationalism and more radical currents. It succeeded for a very short period and ended in isolating the collaborationist layer of landlords and merchants much more rapidly than it had done in India.[19] As Curzon had once

---

19 Isolation took from 1757 to 1947 in India, from 1914 to 1958 in Iraq. Richard Gott's *Our Empire Story* (forthcoming) charts the history of the British Empire and reveals an astonishing statistic: for every single day that this Empire existed there was a corresponding act of rebellion by its subjects against its rule. It is something that the new Empire loyalists might ponder as the situation in Iraq unfolds and US casualties slowly mount.

acidly noted, the victory of the 'wretched Bolsheviks' and their incessant anti-imperialist rants had made the Empire's task much more difficult. The institutionalisation of private estates weakened the traditional tribal structures and, in the regions where this happened, created a class of property-less peasants. In the towns the entry of foreign capital and its embrace by local entrepreneurs created a further class divide and, more dangerously for the imperial authorities, fuelled the rise of a radical nationalism and led to the formation of a Communist Party, which soon became the most influential in the Arab East.

Conceived in the womb of the British Empire, Iraq was formally baptised and adopted by the League of Nations. This august body, created by the victors of the First World War, issued a Mandate granting the British the right to run the country. This reality – it was a colonial state from birth – determined its structures. The Colonial Office in London made all the key military, economic, and foreign policy decisions. Even local disputes related to patronage, ethnicity, or religion were not usually the prerogative of the King and his advisers. The British High Commissioner had to be consulted on matters large and small.[20] Since the monarchy, too, was imposed from above, its legitimacy was under challenge from the very beginning and from every side. Without a halo, the new King had to operate like any other collaborationist politician, while pretending to be above the fray. Feisal knew that most of the former Ottoman officers and bureaucrats who surrounded him were not to be trusted. Each carried his

---

20   Charles Tripp explains that: 'The principal currency of the patronage system was land … for the authorities, therefore, it was a way of purchasing social order. … It had been a feature since the earliest years of the British occupation when Henry Dobbs (revenue commissioner during the military occupation and later high commissioner under the Mandate, 1923–29) saw the confirmation and grant of title to land and the distribution of leases as the most effective means of ensuring order in the countryside.' *A History of Iraq*, Cambridge, 2000, pp. 51–2.

At the Peace Conference in Paris, the Emir Feisal (1885–1933), 'king' of the Hijaz, who became King Feisal I of Iraq (centre). Behind him (l to r) are 'General' Nuri al-Said (1888–1958), an unidentified Anglo-Irish soldier, Captain Pisani of the French Mission, Thomas Edward Shaw (Lawrence of Arabia, 1888–1935), and two unidentified men.

own pack of cards. During the first few years of his reign, Feisal was impressed by the quality of the intelligence assembled by Nuri al-Said, who played the part of fawning protégé to perfection. Later, when Nuri's mask sometimes slipped, the Hashemite Othello became suspicious and increasingly worried by the intrigues of his Baghdadi Iago. During the last years of his reign, Feisal distanced himself from this courtier. He sometimes chafed at British control and wanted a degree of real independence, but he had no real options. The French had booted him out of Damascus. The al-Sauds had defeated his father and taken over Mecca and Medina. The British had, at least, given him a country and a throne. For this he was grateful. He did not like to criticise his benefactor publicly, but when he did the British High Commissioner was unscrupulous in mobilising sections of the Shia to protest against a Sunni ruler. After a short-lived opposition against his patrons, Feisal realised he could never outmanoeuvre the Colonial Office. He knew from the experience of his own family in the Hijaz that there were always other jokers in the imperial pack. Unhappily, he accepted the role he now had to play, declaring bluntly: 'I am an instrument of British policy.'[21] He was hurt, if not surprised, by the fact that for the first three years of his reign the Friday *khutba* in the mosques was begun in the name of the defeated Caliph in Istanbul. How long this might have continued had Kemal Pasha not abolished the Caliphate in 1924 is an open question. What was not in doubt, and Emir Feisal must have reflected on this a great deal, was the grim reality of a colonial state. British control was much stronger and less flexible than that of the Ottomans. Had his family made a mistake in ganging up with the British? If these thoughts crossed his mind he did not share them with his advisers. But were any of his doubts transmitted to his son Ghazi?

By contrast, the actions and behaviour of Iago-Nuri – a central figure in the politics of colonial Iraq – were reminiscent of a medieval Florentine in whose service poisoners might have been encouraged to perfect their art. Who was Nuri al-Said? He was the son of a petty clerk in the service of the Ottomans. Jafar Askari and other fellow cadets, who were later to

---

21   This was the case on most issues and Feisal collaborated to the hilt in the bogus elections for the Constituent Assembly, where favoured toadies were 'elected' in the face of popular opposition. Elections under imperial occupation are rarely free or fair, contrary to the history rewritten by the would-be collaborators of today. There is a revealing and detailed account of what happened during the first colonisation in M. M. al-Adhami's essay, 'The Elections for the Constituent Assembly in Iraq, 1922–24', in *The Integration of Modern Iraq*, edited by Abbas Kelidar, London, 1979.

popperfoto.com.

Nuri al-Said at the first session of the US-sponsored Baghdad Pact, 16 April 1956. The Iago of the first colonial period, Nuri was the most hated politician in Iraq. He was executed after the 1958 revolution.

desert to the Hashemites, also came from lower-middle-class back-grounds. They were trained in the Ottoman military academy in Istanbul where they graduated and became officers in the Sultan's army. In 1916, Sharif Hussein of Mecca, realising that the Ottomans had backed the wrong side, raised the banner of rebellion and joined the British war effort. T.E. Lawrence undoubtedly aided the process but was not as decisive as he claimed. Arab clans rarely needed help when it was time to change sides. From the inside, Nuri al-Said and Jafar Askari also noticed the disintegration of the Ottoman armies. Captured by the British in 1916, the two men were easily persuaded to change sides. When Sharif Hussein declared his support for Britain, the British offered their services to the guardian of the Holy Cities. When Sharif Hussein's youngest boy was offered a new country created from three former Ottoman provinces, the Mesopotamian deserters came with him and rose to high office: all four of them became Prime Ministers of Iraq during the monarchy. Nuri was driven largely by personal ambition but also by a desire to prove something to the local notables who complained to the King about the company he kept, especially the officers who surrounded him, hailing as they did from a 'third class of people'. Not the lowest of the low, but low Nuri was determined to rise high above his detractors. And, as far as wealth was concerned, he achieved this aim.

His primary loyalty was to himself and the carefully knit cabal of sycophants with which he surrounded himself. To preserve his position he became the tried, if not completely trusted, friend of the British. Corrupt, ruthless, intoxicated with power, proximity to which for him became a vital psycho-economic need, Nuri al-Said soon became a much-despised political figure. He was perceived on the street as a shameless manipulator, and hatred of him often united the people of Iraq. The merchants, who were the key social layer in Baghdad and Basrah during the early days of the monarchy, always regarded Nuri and the other politicians with utter contempt. Years later, a businessman informed a visiting historian that politicians like Nuri and his gang were corrupt to the core, they were 'dogs and one best deals with dogs by tossing bones to them'.[22]

This type of unpopularity rarely bothered him. It was being out of favour with the court or the British that reduced Nuri al-Said to a state of 'nervous excitement'. He became obsessive, plotting endless scenarios with one ending: his own speedy return to power. Invariably, this addiction

---

22   *The Old Social Classes and the Revolutionary Movements of Iraq: A Study of Iraq's Old Landed and Commercial Classes and of its Communists, Ba'athists and Free Officers*, by Hanna Batatu, Princeton, 1978.

to power led to an overdose of intrigue. In case his plans went awry, which they did, a packed suitcase was always ready to aid a quick getaway. He never had to search hard for a safe refuge. A spare bedroom in the British Embassy was usually available as a temporary haven. When the situation deteriorated further, making his presence in Baghdad temporarily impossible, he was rushed to the airport and put on the next flight to either Cairo or London. Here he was encouraged to relax and detoxify, but Nuri could not break the habit. Nor did he try. He was in a state of permanent readiness, preparing his return and mapping the contours of the next power struggle.

Feisal's death in 1933 appeared to provide the first opportunity. Ghazi, the new king, was twenty-one years old when he took his father's place. He was reputed to be weak, debauched, and malleable, easily influenced by the views of the last courtier he had met. At least this is what Nuri al-Said wanted everyone to believe and it is what his cabal told the British. It was a serious case of misjudgement. It soon became clear that Ghazi was in tune with the radical nationalist currents that had emerged in Iraq. He was hostile to the British, loathed Nuri al-Said as well as his rival Yasin al-Hashemi, the Prime Minister – a corrupt but capable political operator who, after zigzagging a great deal, had finally thrown in his lot with the British. Yasin had flirted with republicanism and, for that reason alone, was distrusted by Feisal. The latter had not understood that Yasin liked to haggle, and like most of his colleagues, he, too, could be bought.[23] Ghazi's political aversion to Yasin was no different from the hatred he felt for Nuri. But the personal loathing stemmed from the Prime Minister's insistence, expressed in diplomatic but unmistakable language, that the King abandon an affair he was having with a pretty manservant. This followed a public scandal in

---

23 Of Yasin the Iraqi poet Ma'ruf ar-Rasafi wrote the following couplet: In his line of vision lies only his personal gain, / It is his guide in all things.

King Ghazi of Iraq, September 1933. The most innovative member of the Hashemite clan, Ghazi set up an anti-imperialist radio station inside the palace. The tone of the broadcasts upset the British and their Kuwaiti protégé. London ordered his deposition. Nuri al-Said, according to the popular view, had him killed. Officially, he died in a car crash. The car was virtually undamaged.

© Hulton-Deutsch Collection/CORBIS

1936, when Ghazi's sister, Princess Azzah, eloped with a Greek hotel waiter from Rhodes and abandoned Islam. *Hic Rhodus, hic salta.*

That Ghazi was headstrong, spoilt, and promiscuous is beyond dispute, but these characteristics are hardly uncommon in ruling or elite families. It was his consistently anti–British stance that led to Yasin's direct pressure on him. The King had set up his own radio station in the palace (a Radio al-Jazeera), which regularly denounced Anglo–Zionist machinations in Palestine; insisted that Kuwait was part of Iraq and appealed to the people of Kuwait to topple the Sheikh; and spoke warmly of the old Berlin to Baghdad railway project, disrupted by the First World War, implying that it should be resumed. The British Ambassador regarded all this as 'total irresponsibility', a mild rebuke given the circumstances, but it was intended only for public consumption.

The King now attempted to use nationalist elements in the army to oust his pro-British ministers. The Mandate had expired in 1929 and with it the direct control of the Colonial Office. The British still dominated the country economically and militarily, but local oligarchs now enjoyed a much larger margin of manoeuvre. Yasin used his brother, Taha (Chief of General Staff), to ensure that their faction received due recognition when appointments were being made in the army as well as the educational sector. This was designed to establish their control over the army and to weaken rival oligarchs Nuri al-Said and Jafar Askari.

Ghazi pre-empted both factions by encouraging General Bakr Sidqi of the First Division, dominated by Kurdish officers, to strike a blow against Yasin and Nuri by marching to Baghdad. This, the first of many coup d'états in Iraqi history, succeeded in toppling the government, but also aroused rival currents and groups embedded inside the army. A year later, four nationalist colonels from petty bourgeois urban backgrounds defeated Bakr Sidqi and reasserted pan-Arab control over the army and the state. With Ghazi's support, they made it clear that they were not prepared to tolerate continuing British interference in the internal affairs of Iraq. With both monarch and army in a recalcitrant mood, how would the Empire and its local factotums react?

The status quo ante was to be restored via a change of kings. Ghazi conveniently died in a car crash, but the circumstances were such that neither the Colonels nor the people believed it was an accident. The pro-British version was that he had crashed his sports car into a lamppost and died instantaneously. But on inspection, it appeared that neither the post nor the car was seriously damaged in this supposedly violent crash. Moreover the servant and the wireless operator, who were also in the car, disappeared without trace, feeding a popular belief that the King had been murdered. Large, emotional crowds attended Ghazi's funeral. The main chant at the event, as reported in a despatch to London, left little room for ambiguity: 'You will answer for the blood of Ghazi, O Nuri!'[24] But were the rumours true? The view that Nuri had organised the murder, in concert with Ghazi's estranged wife Queen Aliyah and her brother Prince Abdul-Ilah, was not simply confined to the Baghdad street. Many in the elite believed this to be the case and some went further to suggest that Ghazi had been murdered with British connivance. The monarch change was far too convenient to be an accident. All that can be said here is that no definitive proof emerged either to substantiate or disprove this thesis.[25]

In his epic history of pre-Saddam Iraq, Hanna Batatu remained unconvinced by the 'accident' version of Ghazi's sudden death. He wrote that 'doubts still surround the incident' and argued that while the British, till January 1939, appeared not to be in favour of removing Ghazi from the throne, 'they may have had a change of heart subsequently.' The King's radio station had intensified its appeal to anti-British nationalism and was urging Kuwaitis to dump their Sheikh and rejoin Iraq. The King himself feared 'imminent assassination' and, as Batatu records, he was not alone:

---

24   FO 371/23201/E2820/72/93, letter of 11 April 1939 from Mr Houston-Boswall, Baghdad, to Viscount Halifax.

25   In his autobiography, Maurice Peterson, the British Ambassador at the time, does not conceal his antipathy to the young king. The combination of Ghazi's homosexuality and his anti-imperialist views was abhorrent to the British in Iraq. Peterson writes: 'That King Ghazi must either be controlled or deposed had become obvious and I hinted as much in a farewell visit I paid to Emir Abdul-Ilah, the present Regent. The solution, had I but known it, lay only a short month ahead. I was sitting in the Condestable Hotel at Burgos when an English journalist told me that King Ghazi, driving as usual his own sports car, had dashed himself to death against a telegraph pole. A pitiful life, pitifully ended. German propaganda tried to saddle us with responsibility for his death. Baghdad was for some days in a ferment and the British Consul in Mosul was murdered by the mob.' The latter was the clearest indication that popular opinion did hold the British responsible even if Nuri and Abdul-Ilah actually organised the murder.

'I remember,' writes ex-Premier Tawfiq as-Suwaidi, 'the meeting I had [two weeks before Ghazi's death] with R. Butler, the Permanent Under Secretary for Foreign Affairs. He told me that the King was playing with fire and feared that His Majesty might burn his fingers.' More importantly, a few days or so later Butler discussed with Ambassador Maurice Peterson 'the relative merits' of the various members of the royal house 'in case any emergency might arise'... The lurking suspicion of having masterminded or played roles as accessories to outside influences in the King's death pursued Nuri, Abdul-Ilah, and Queen Aliyah to the end of their lives, and was one of the elements that damaged the moral authority of the Crown beyond repair.'[26]

The first three decades of the monarchic–imperial regime were an unmitigated disaster for the local people. The cost of imposing the colonial regime and an outside monarch was high: the use of chemical weapons and air power had led to 98,000 casualties. And there was savage political repression at home symbolised by public hangings: one of those dealt with in such a fashion was the communist leader Fahd. The number of people killed in the period 1920-48 was extremely high when compared, for instance, to colonial India. And critical estimates of British rule in Iraq were not confined to nationalist or leftwing writers. The balance-sheet offered by Elie Kedourie, a historian not known for his sympathy to empires, was in this case wholly negative. Kedourie wrote of Hashemite Iraq as a despotism reliant on the coercive powers of the British Empire,

---

26 Batatu, op cit, pp. 342–44. This is an amazing book on every level. Apart from the quality of his own scholarship, Batatu's access to the police files in Baghdad, his meticulous study of British Foreign Office documents, and the interviews he conducted with many of the leading figures who were still alive (including imprisoned communists) make this a unique study of the country. Dozens of books on Iraq have appeared since, but none of them comes even close to matching Batatu's scholarship or his detachment.

Hanna Batatu (1926–2000), Emeritus Professor at Georgetown University, whose two classic studies of Iraq and Syria are crucial in understanding the present. Batatu's telling comparison of US and Ba'athist politicians – both equally remote from the people – symbolised the independence of his thought (see footnote 59 on p. 112).

and inaugurating a period 'full of bloodshed, treason and rapine' whose end was 'implicit in its beginning'.[27]

The British authorities themselves were highly critical of the regimes sustained by them. In November 1943, the British Ambassador, Cornwallis, wrote to Anthony Eden in the Foreign Office, explaining how he had confronted Nuri 'for the manner in which they have tolerated dishonesty ... for corruption in the police, the unreliability of the army, the mishandling of the Kurds, the shameless landgrabbing carried on by prominent personalities ... and the wide gulf between the government and the people'. When the British Intelligence Service accurately referred to the government as 'an oligarchy of racketeers', Cornwallis became slightly defensive: 'It is going altogether too far to describe them indiscriminately as crooks.'[28] It was an intractable problem. These were the only people in Iraq who supported the Empire.

The murder/death of Ghazi accelerated pan-Arab nationalism, and in 1941 the coup of the Four Colonels installed a popular nationalist

---

27 Elie Kedourie, *The Chatham House Version and Other Middle-Eastern Studies*, London, 1970.
28 Batatu, op cit, p. 347.

government, which attempted to establish relations with both Berlin and Moscow. The Regent, Abdul-Ilah, and Nuri fled the country. A thirty-day war ensued and the British legions reoccupied Iraq. Their task was made easier by Hitler's invasion of the Soviet Union, which divided the anti-imperialist movement in Iraq as in India and other British, French, and Dutch colonies. The nationalists refused to collaborate with their occupiers; the communists reluctantly followed Moscow and ceased all effective opposition. Nonetheless, throughout the war years and after, the cauldron continued to simmer. The pro-British elite never fully understood the extent of its own isolation.[29] Only this could explain the provocation mounted by Nuri and the hated Hashemite regent Abdul-Ilah, to secretly renegotiate the 1930 Treaty with Britain and present it to Iraqis as a fait accompli.[30] The Portsmouth Agreement of 1948 was a continuation of the old arrangements under a new name. News that it was being negotiated sparked off the first demonstrations in early January of that year. Secondary school students who came out to protest were joined by students from the Law School. As the demonstration swelled it was confronted and clubbed by mounted policemen. Later the police fired bullets and several students were felled. The next day every single college and school came out on strike. The government released all the arrested students and a tense calm prevailed for the next two weeks.

---

29   It was as if dressing like the British and obeying their orders were enough to stay in power. The fourteenth-century Arab historian had occasion to remark on this phenomenon: 'The vanquished always seek to imitate their victors in their dress, insignia, belief and other customs and usages ... they do so because they refuse to admit that their defeat could have been brought about by ordinary causes, and hence they suppose it is due to the perfection of the conquerors.' Ibn Khaldun, *Prolegomena*, vol. 1, p. 266.

30   The 1930 Treaty reduced Iraq to the status of a de facto British Protectorate, allowing the Empire permanent military bases and reducing the port town of Basrah (currently occupied by British troops) and Iraqi Railways into corporations run by British administrators.

At this stage the Iraqi Communist Party (of which more in the following chapter) decided to enter the fray. It mobilised the railway workers and the city poor to join the students in a massive march on 20 January. The police were ordered to open fire and several demonstrators were killed. This triggered a mass uprising, unprecedented even for this country with its past of continuous rebellion. People had lost all fear and the following day large crowds took over the city. The movement was now referred to as *al-wathbah* ('the leap') to signify the leap in mass consciousness that had taken place over the preceding forty-eight hours. At first the police continued to fire, killing two students in the Medicine Faculty. This raised the temperature and there were rumblings inside the army. As the situation spiralled out of control, the Regent called an emergency meeting at the palace where the liberal parties were invited. He agreed to disown the Portsmouth treaty.

The masses could not be demobilised that easily. The liberal groups pleaded for understanding and more time for 'his highness', but the crowd wanted more, and slogans in favour of 'Free bread for all' and 'the Republic' were heard in the poorer quarters. On 27 January the government fully embraced modernity and civilisation: it ordered armoured cars and machine-guns to deal with the crowd. The mood now became insurrectionary. An armoured car was burnt. The authorities were determined to prevent people linking up across the Ma'mun Bridge, and the machine-gun detachments opened fire. Hundreds were killed that day, but despite the bodies that floated down the Tigris, people continued to move forward. A fifteen-year-old girl, carrying a banner and surrounded by four of her friends, defied the machine-guns. With heads erect they began to cross the bridge. As she walked, her four comrades fell to the ground, mowed down by bullets. She reached the other side. Her courage spurred the others. People began to regroup and advance. At this stage the police, shaken by the determination of the crowd, retreated completely. The streets became liberated zones. That same night the Prime Minister, Salih Jabr – a Nuri protégé – fled Baghdad in fear. At first he went south to the Euphrates, later he sought and was granted exile in Britain. The movement continued for another four months, but *al-wathbah* was about to be overtaken by the *nakba* in Palestine. The satraps hijacked the genuine anger of the people against the Zionists as they prepared to wage a phoney war against the new state of Israel. Using this new danger as a cover, a severe repression was mounted against the Iraqi communists. Fahd, the leader of the Communist Party, had been in prison throughout *al-wathbah*. He was now charged with having led the party from prison. Together with two other members of the leadership – Zaki Basim and ash-Shabibi – he was brought before a special tribunal. All three were found guilty and hanged.

Yusuf Salman Yusuf, a communist of Christian origin, adopted the name Fahd in the underground. He was secretary general of Iraqi Communist Party from 1941 to 1948. Fahd and other communist leaders were arrested in 1947. After the semi-insurrection against the colonial regime in 1948, he was re-tried and executed in secret. His body and that of his comrade Zaki Yasin were hung from lampposts to terrorise the population. Fahd was the only communist leader of the Arab world to oppose the Soviet recognition of Israel.

Their bodies were strung up in three public squares as a warning to others who sought to challenge the state. What the rulers of Iraq could never imagine was that the hangings and *al-wathbah* were a deadly dress rehearsal for a future in which the roles would be reversed.

With Iraq once again occupied by Western powers, a study of this phase in Iraqi history is hardly a diversion. There is an additional reason for the detour. During the peak of Saddam's repressive dictatorship – 1980–89 – when he was receiving valuable support from Washington and London in crushing local opposition and waging war against Iran, a mood of despair gripped many Iraqi exiles. A few launched their own revolt against history by viewing the Hashemite period nostalgically. In contradistinction to the views expressed by British imperial administrators of the period, the years of the Hashemite monarchy were seen by some as a golden age. Appended to this was a grotesque idealisation of Emir Feisal as a liberal moderniser, a view that would have made many of his own courtiers cringe with embarrassment. This imagined past led Kanaan Makiya to call for a permanent US occupation of Iraq (on the Japanese model) during the First Gulf War and subsequently to support the invasion and recolonisation of 2003.[31] The exiles' despair led to political neurosis and attachment to an old-new dogma: civilisation versus barbarism. All else had failed. Hope, for the converts to imperialism, now lay in the forward march of the American Empire.

---

31   The Anglo-Iraqi professor Kanaan Makiya is a leading member of the new imperial freemasonry. His *Republic of Fear*, London, 1989 (written under a nom-de-plume), marked his evolution from Marxist to liberal-imperialist. Like his fellow professor Fouad Ajmi, he is feted in liberal circles for 'explaining' the Arab world to the West and justifying US foreign policy. One of the more effective critiques of Makiya can be found in Peter Gowan's essay 'The Gulf War and Western Liberalism', in *The Global Gamble*, London, 1999, pp. 141–86.

4

COLONELS AND COMMUNISTS

The year 1958 was the high noon of Arab nationalism. The popularity of Gamal Abdel Nasser, who symbolised the new mood, had risen to new heights in the Arab East and the Maghreb, threatening to sweep aside the old order. What worried the satraps was that support for the Egyptian leader transcended ethnic, sectarian, and religious divides. Nor was it confined to the Arab street. Inside each Arab army there existed secret societies of 'patriotic officers'. They regarded the political revolution in Egypt as a victory for the Arab nation. Likewise Nasser's triple triumph: the nationalisation of the Suez Canal; the reassertion of Egyptian national sovereignty after the retreat of the Anglo-French-Israeli armies that had invaded in 1956; and the Soviet Union's agreement to fund the Aswan Dam after the West withdrew its support. A wave of pride swept the region, encouraging a rebellious mood in Algeria and Syria, Saudi Arabia and Tunisia, Jordan and Morocco, Palestinian refugee camps and the Lebanon.

And Iraq? Here, a nervous elite had decided that the only path to survival was through large-scale internal repression, supported by foreign powers. When the country was not under martial law, political freedoms were very tightly restricted by royal decree. This suited both the US and Britain. So confident were they in Hashemite stability that in 1959 they decided to name a new security arrangement the Baghdad Pact, the aim

Gamal Abdel Nasser.

of which was to establish a network of military bases to secure the oil wealth of the region and to keep the communist enemy at bay. This was the Portsmouth treaty writ large and with a powerful new guarantor: the United States.

It was also a challenge to the opposition, but the communists refused to swallow the bait. They knew that the public was not prepared for a new mass movement, and an economic boom had led to a small rise in living standards. Their refusal to launch a movement at this time encouraged Nuri al-Said to imprison or banish any Iraqi convicted of harbouring communist sympathies and, in 1955, to break off all relations with the Soviet Union. In the previous year, Nuri had organised an election after dissolving his own party and repressing his non-communist rivals.

Out of the 135 deputies 116 were elected unopposed and, with this majority, Nuri effectively banned all political parties and restricted the right to organise and attend public meetings. The stage was now set for the Baghdad Pact. Its members were Britain, Turkey, Iran, Iraq, and Pakistan. Washington thought it prudent to remain in the background and the minutes of the first meeting coyly noted: 'also present, on invitation to the first meeting of the Baghdad Pact Council, Baghdad, Nov. 21–22, 1955, were two observers from the United States [Ambassador Waldemar J. Gallman and Admiral John H. Cassady].' The new security arrangement angered pan-Arab nationalists. From Cairo, Nasser denounced the treaty as an infringement of Arab sovereignty. Political activities in Iraq were heavily curtailed, but it was not so simple to keep a permanent watch inside the army.

Nasser's supporters and others inside the Iraqi army were organised clandestinely as the 'Free Officers', and after the Suez war of 1956 (during which the Baghdad Pact states supported the Anglo-French-Israeli invasion of Egypt), their numbers grew and attempts by Nuri to track them down and disperse them were only partially successful. The Iraqi Communist Party, too, had cells inside the army. These were well-trained and organised cadres skilled in underground activities. The third force was the fledgling Ba'ath Party based largely in the south and under the leadership of Fuad al-Rikabi, a young engineer from Nasiriyah. The Ba'ath had considerable success in winning over young Shias critical of clerics and landowners. It, too, maintained a few cells inside the army.

The officer corps of the Iraqi army had, since the opening of the Military College to universal applications in 1934, become the only institution in the country where virtually every segment of society was represented. As in Egypt, the removal of restrictions on officer recruitment led to a large influx of cadets from urban petty-bourgeois families. This was done largely under the pressure of the Palace. It went against the grain of British imperial thinking, which was ultra-cautious on these matters and preserved a strict class hierarchy when creating a colonial army in India or Africa. But Nuri al-Said and his cronies, for their own reasons, which were not unrelated to their own social and class backgrounds, wanted to create an army whose composition transcended regional, ethnic, and tribal divisions and which, they assumed, would become a loyal instrument of the monarchy and help to create a new Iraqi identity. Soldiers were recruited from town and country were Sunni and Shia, Kurd and Arab, Chaldean and Circassian. But the best-laid plans of satrap and servant are often disrupted by history. And so it came about that many intelligent young men attracted to radical ideas decided to join the army, something that was inconceivable in India during the same period. It was in the army that the barrier between town and country gradually disappeared. Ironically, the army did become the crucible in which a new Iraqi identity was forged, but this was done by excluding the monarchy and seeing Iraq as part of a wider entity that was the Arab nation. It was only after the defeat of Arab nationalism that the sub-nationalisms tied to the new states developed an identity that was largely their own.

All the political currents inside the army were angered by the Baghdad Pact and its implications. In February 1957 the liberal, nationalist, and communist parties had grouped together under the umbrella of a United National Front to challenge Nuri and the palace. The military supporters of this Front were now instructed to think seriously of permanently removing the 'oligarchy of racketeers' from power. The Supreme Committee of the Free Officers consisted of twelve officers. Sandwiched between a brigadier and a major were ten colonels, graduates of the Iraq Military Academy during the late thirties. What united them? A vague dislike of landowners, a strong hostility to the corrupt clique centred on the Palace/Nuri axis, and a deep hatred of the British Empire. In 1957 the Supreme Committee set up a number of sub-committees to plan the uniformed revolution. They were determined to win over the commanders of all the major military units. This led them to approach Brigadier Abdul-Karim Qasim, whose own background – he was the son of a Sunni carpenter and a Kurdish-Shia mother – appeared to symbolise the unity of Iraq. The Free Officers were delighted to discover that Qasim had already organised a group of younger nationalist-minded officers, and the merger of the two groups meant that all the senior commanding officers were now in one organisation. Qasim was made Chairman of the Supreme Committee by virtue of his seniority. As news of this trickled out to the political parties, they instructed their supporters to join the Free Officers group, a move not universally welcomed by the military dissidents, some of who were hostile to all politicians.[32]

In February 1958, the Syrian Ba'athists and Nasser had agreed to the unity of Syria and Egypt and formed the United Arab Republic (UAR). The declared aim was to lay the foundations of Arab Unity and isolate the pro-Western regimes. An unstated reason was to marginalise the influence of the Arab Communist Parties. In Syria, for instance, it was generally accepted that the Ba'ath Party would not win power at the next general election and might even be eclipsed by the Syrian communists. The Syrian Ba'ath leader Salah Bitar and the party's founder and chief ideologue Michel Aflaq rushed to Cairo to push through the founding of the UAR in the full knowledge that one consequence of the union would be the permanent cancellation of the Syrian elections.

To the outside world the formation of the UAR was seen either as a massive leap forward in the direction of a fully fledged Arab Unity or as a threat to the status quo. In Baghdad, Nuri al-Said and his British masters concocted a counter-union. The Arab Union united the twin Hashemite monarchies of Iraq and Jordan with Nuri al-Said as its first Prime Minister. Kuwait was intended as the third member of this short-lived union, which might have led to interesting consequences, but before the British could attach the Sheikh of Kuwait's thumbprint to the treaty (if they ever agreed to it) there was an unexpected interruption. A revolution had erupted in Iraq.

The Free Officers had taken every possible precaution. In April an emissary had visited Cairo to meet Nasser, inform him of their plans and

---

32 Interestingly, Qasim and two other members of the Supreme Committee had been trained at the Senior Officers School in Devizes; another two had served time at the British Staff College in Camberley. The experience was put to good use in 1958.

request help in the event that the West used the Baghdad Pact to invade Iraq. The Egyptian leader pledged all-out and unconditional support. In return the Supreme Committee unanimously agreed that if the Baghdad Pact powers invaded Iraq, it would join the UAR with immediate effect. Amazingly none of these moves reached British intelligence. All they received were the soothing despatches from the Ambassador who, moving exclusively in elite circles, wrote that the situation was stable.

On 14 July 1958 the Free Officers seized power and declared Iraq a Republic. At 6.30 a.m. the first proclamation was read on Radio Baghdad by Colonel Aref, who informed the country that

> with the loyal aid of the loyal sons of the people and the national armed forces, we have undertaken to liberate the beloved homeland from the corrupt crew that imperialism installed. Brethren, the army is of you and for you and has carried out what you desired … your duty is to support it in the wrath that it is pouring on the Rihab Palace and the house of Nuri al-Said. Only by preserving it from the plots of imperialism and its stooges can victory be brought to completion …[33]

The military leaders had planned to exile the young king Feisal II, but to arrest and try his uncle, the Crown Prince Abdul-Ilah, and Nuri al-Said for crimes against the people. Plans had been made to carry out the verdicts without delay. Obviously they would have been found guilty and executed, but all this was pre-empted by a young officer. He had been completely unaware of the planned coup. After he heard Aref's radio broadcast, he joined the rebellion. As one of the emissaries negotiating

---

33 Batatu, op cit. The book contains the most complete and documented account of the Iraqi revolution of 1958 and its aftermath, ending on the eve of Saddam Hussein's assumption of total power in 1979.

the surrender of the Palace Guard he entered the palace. When he saw the royal family assembling in the courtyard, he lost control and began to fire machine-gun bullets in their direction. At this point other soldiers opened fire. When the firing ceased, the King, his uncle, and some officers lay dead. Nuri al-Said did not wait to be arrested. He disguised himself as a woman and attempted to escape, but the British Embassy was no longer safe and was, in any case, surrounded by angry crowds. Before Nuri could leave the city, he was recognised and apprehended. An air force sergeant executed him on the spot. The next day the body of Abdul-Ilah was disinterred and hung from a lamppost at the entrance to the old Ministry of Defence at the exact spot where he had hanged Colonel Salah al-din-al-Sabaq, a popular leader of the 1941 revolt. The bodies were then cut into pieces as if they were sacrificial lambs and burnt. This was the supreme insult: the dead men were denied a Muslim burial. When the end finally came no section of the army or the population was prepared to defend the old regime. It was this reality that made any foreign intervention an impossibility.

The nationalist groups and the Communist Party had been told of the date of the coup. They had, accordingly, alerted their supporters, but as news swept the country, the excited crowds that poured out on the streets of Baghdad, Basrah, Nasiriyah, Kirkuk, and Mosul to celebrate the triumph swamped the members of political parties. The descriptions of the event speak of these spontaneous mass mobilisations as 'overflowing rivers', 'tides that engulfed', 'purifying floods'. The popularity of the revolution was unquestionable. In Baghdad, over a hundred thousand people tore down the statue of Emir Feisal. The same fate befell the stone effigy of General Maude, the 'conqueror of Baghdad', situated conveniently in front of the old British Chancellery, which was set on fire, providing a dramatic backdrop to the symbolic execution of the British general. Far from being orchestrated, these unprompted displays of joy, anger, hatred, and revenge seriously worried the military leaders, who feared they might lose control of the situation. The Revolutionary Council hurriedly proclaimed a curfew to get people off the streets. And yet it was their support that provided the legitimacy for the military take-over. The overthrow of the monarchy had been accomplished by a total of no more than 3,000 soldiers, most of whom had no ammunition. Of course other units could have been summoned, but if the streets had remained empty the monarchists and their Baghdad Pact allies might have been emboldened to resist. Hanna Batatu stresses the logistic, political, and psychological importance of popular mobilisation:

> the ruthlessness with which at least some of them proceeded to give vent to their feelings must have had a greater weight in determining the historical outcome of that fateful day than one might at first glance be disposed to admit. ... For one thing, by clogging streets and bridges not only in Baghdad but other towns, it hindered possible hostile counteractions. More than that, by virtue of its vehemence, it had a tremendous psychological impact. It planted fear in the heart of the supporters of the monarchy, and helped to paralyse their will and give the coup the irresistible character that was its surest bulwark.[34]

The new Iraqi regime was confronted with a set of choices and problems on both domestic and external fronts. At home, twenty-three families − the Chalabis, Pachachis, al-Khudaivis, et al. − controlled 56 percent of the private commercial and industrial capital of the country. The oil was under the control of the British-owned Iraq Petroleum

---

34 Batatu, op cit, p. 805. This view countered that of the US Ambassador, Waldemar J. Gallman, who refused to acknowledge the popularity of the coup, insisting that the crowds were 'not representative Iraqis but hoodlums recruited by agitators'. The epic struggle by the United States to find 'representative Iraqis' continues to this day.

Company.[35] In the countryside the British had transformed the tribal sheikhs into owners of large estates,[36] thus creating a material basis for long-term collaboration on a model tried and tested in the South Asian subcontinent: like their counterparts in Sind and Bengal the Iraqi peasants became virtual serfs. Higher education was largely a preserve of the upper and middle classes. There were obvious solutions to these problems and over the next decade they were satisfactorily resolved. Key industries, including oil, were nationalised; radical agrarian reforms broke the back of landlordism; children (boys and girls) from poor families began to receive a proper education and gender discrimination began to be seriously tackled.

---

35 'The Iraq Petroleum Company Limited was incorporated in 1911 as the African and Eastern Concessions Limited. Its name was changed to the Turkish Petroleum Company Limited in 1912, and to the Iraq Petroleum Company Limited in 1929. By the San Remo Oil Agreement of 1920, the shareholding in the Company was arranged as Anglo-Persian Oil Company Limited (47.5 percent), Shell (22.5 percent), Compagnie Française des Pétroles (25 percent), and C. S. Gulbenkian (5 percent). A concession was obtained in 1925 and oil was first struck by the Company in 1927. In 1928 the Red Line Agreement was signed after much debate between the groups. It rearranged the shareholding as follows: Anglo-Persian Oil Company Limited (23.75 percent), Shell (23.75 percent), Compagnie Française des Pétroles (23.75 percent), the Near East Development Corporation (23.75 percent), and Gulbenkian (5 percent). The Concession Agreement was revised in 1931. The 1928 Red Line Agreement was superseded by a Revised Group Agreement in 1948. The wholly owned subsidiaries of Basrah Petroleum Company Limited and Mosul Petroleum Company Limited obtained further concessions in 1938 and 1942 respectively. Pipelines to the Mediterranean were completed in the 1930s and 1940s. The company also acquired significant interests in Middle Eastern concessions outside Iraq.' This is a limited but accurate self-portrait by the IPC. In 1961 the new regime brought these arrangements to an end and some years later the oil was nationalised. Today in the era of capitalist banditry described by polite people as 'globalisation' the United States' occupation of Iraq will privatise the commodity once again. And twenty years from now?
36 Thus Major Pulley reporting to the Civil Commissioner in Baghdad on 6 August 1920: 'Many of them were small men of no account until we made them powerful and rich.' These British-made sheikhs in Iraq remained loyal to the colonial order till the end. Their parasitic status in Iraq has been well documented and analysed by Marion Farouk-Sluglett and Peter Sluglett, *Iraq Since 1958: From Revolution to Dictatorship*, London, 1987.

What posed an intractable difficulty was politics. How and by whom should Iraq be governed? In the Arab world itself there were two basic models: pro-Western monarchies, sheikhdoms, and colonies (like Algeria and Aden), and anti-Western populist-military regimes. Lebanon was the only semi-democracy based on an institutionalised power-sharing between the Christian and Muslim elites. In the world at large there were the following models: Western-style capitalist democracies; the swathe of US-backed military dictatorships in Latin America as well as the member states of the Baghdad Pact, Iran, Turkey, and Pakistan; and lastly the non-capitalist one-party states typified by the Soviet Union, China, Vietnam, and North Korea. The Western model (or a variant that allowed for representative institutions while outlawing the obscene use of money or property) was rejected by all three leading players in post-revolutionary Iraq.

Qasim modelled himself on Nasser, but kept the UAR at arm's length. The Iraqi Communist Party supported him because they were against Iraq joining the UAR as it was constituted at the time. They favoured an Arab federation composed of autonomous, sovereign units with a common foreign and defence policy. If Nasser and the Ba'ath had accepted this model, they might have enlarged and preserved the UAR. But neither party trusted the Arab Communist Parties not because they were communists, but because they operated as Moscow's instruments in the region. The two major complaints of Arab nationalists against the communists were that: (a) they had ceased all opposition to the French and British occupying armies during the Second World War, and (b) they had gone against all their own political instincts and the advice of their own Jewish members and backed the formation of Israel because this was official Soviet policy at the time.

As to the first charge the communists pleaded guilty. They argued that the defeat of fascism was the central task facing the world, but when asked why this had become central only after Hitler's invasion of the USSR in August 1941, they fell silent.[37] With regard to Israel they admitted it had been a serious mistake. But the divisions between these two political currents were never resolved and both Nasser and the Ba'ath at various times brutally repressed the communists. The failure of all three groups to support the existence of a genuine assembly and the right of other political parties to exist, meant that all of them suffered. The lack of institutions in which these and other political divisions could be discussed and presented to the people at large paved the way for personal dictatorships in Egypt, Syria, and Iraq.

The political formation of the nationalist colonels had taken place inside the army, a hierarchical structure *par excellence*. The colonels were used to receiving and giving orders. The questioning of instructions was not permitted. This style of operation slipped into politics. Nasser, like a previous Egyptian reformer (Mohammed Ali), was a great admirer of Napoleon, whose temporary occupation of Egypt in 1798 was viewed locally as non-exploitative.[38] And a century and a half later, Bonapartism

---

37   A similar argument had taken place in colonial India, pitting nationalists against communists. While the latter were released from prisons to help the war effort their nationalist counterparts were arrested for demanding that the British 'Quit India.' Jawaharlal Nehru, the left-nationalist leader, informed the British that India alone should choose whether it wanted its people to die in a European war. He would argue in favour of the anti-fascist alliance, but what he objected to was the pressganging of his country without any consultation with the popular representatives. The Arab Communist Parties, unlike Nehru, dropped the demand for independence during the war. The Syrian Communist leader, Khaled Bakhdash, abased himself before the French to such a degree that it alienated him completely from other Arab leaders and even some communists.

38   According to Arab historians, it was French orientalists accompanying Napoleon who first translated the word 'republic' into Arabic as 'jumhur'. One of the more interesting accounts of Napoleon's impact on Egypt is contained in Ibrahim Abu-Lughod, *Arab Rediscovery of Europe: A Study in Cultural Encounters*, Princeton, 1963. If this is the case, a puzzle remains: how and why did Arab historians of the ninth and tenth centuries, who had access to Greek and Roman classics which were regularly translated into Arabic, fail to translate this particular word.

– which raised the solitary leader above social classes and politics – became the religion of military-populists throughout the Arab world and elsewhere. Despite Nasser's enormous popularity in Egypt and the mythic status he enjoyed elsewhere in the Muslim world, the overall effect of this style of politics was dire. The legacy was poisoned.

In Iraq the military regime soon became enmeshed in a series of severe factional struggles. The lack of serious institutions in which differences could be discussed and debated meant that different factions fought for control of the army, whose Council of Commanders was the only institution that really mattered. In classic Bonapartist fashion, Qasim sometimes used the communists as a buffer against Nasser and the Ba'ath and turned viciously against them when they became too demanding. Nasser's hostility to the Iraqi leader was based on what he perceived to be an over-dependence on the Iraqi Communist Party. Qasim's deputy, Abdus Salam Aref, was a pure Nasserite. He wanted the merger of Iraq with the UAR and was happy to accept Nasser as the supreme leader. Strategically and politically this made a great deal of sense. An expanded UAR was the only route to its survival. It would have weakened Egyptian control and compelled Cairo to a compromise settlement with Damascus and Baghdad. But both Qasim and Nasser stubbornly refused to compromise – Qasim because he knew he could not compete with the man in Cairo and he was fearful of being sidelined or displaced; Nasser because he knew the Iraqi people were behind him and this knowledge enhanced his arrogance. Both men were aware that the crowds in Baghdad had not chanted the name of Qasim, but instead cried, 'We are your soldiers, Gamal Abdel Nasser. Your soldiers!' Nonetheless Nasser insisted that the Iraqi revolution should consolidate itself before moving outwards. He was in favour of unity, but the timing had to be carefully chosen. On the surface this was also Qasim's view, but the mood on the Iraqi streets was extremely volatile. Pan-Arab sentiment was at its height and the political intervention of the Ba'athists centred on the demand for unity with Nasser, if not today, then definitely tomorrow. They were not prepared to wait too long.

To add to the pressure, Michel Aflaq, the Secretary-General and founder of the Ba'ath Party, decided not to waste any time. In 1957, the Ba'ath's membership in Iraq was less than five hundred. It grew in 1958, but at the time of the revolution, contrary to party mythology, it was still under a thousand. This did not bother Aflaq in the slightest. In Syria, he had built his sect into a party by exploiting communist weaknesses, infiltrating the army, clinging to Nasser's prestige and that of the anti-imperialist Syrian deputy Akram Hourani. It had been a fairly successful operation. Ten days after the revolution, Aflaq arrived in Baghdad and calmly informed the people that since they had always been supporters of Arab unity, they must not now permit any vacillation by the faint-hearted. Aflaq's mystical belief in the Arab nation was reiterated once again for the benefit of Iraqis: the 'mission' to be fulfilled by the Arab nation 'does not cease because Arab nationalism is life itself'. The Ba'ath cadres were told to continue the struggle for Arab unity in the name of Nasser and Aref.

The Ba'ath leader had recognised a potential recruit in the second most important figure of the revolution. Since Aref's own political beliefs were dominated by the single idea of Arab unity, he did not need too much persuasion from Aflaq. He toured the country, addressing giant crowds and stoking their passions yet further. In all these speeches Nasser was 'our hero', 'the great liberator', 'our elder brother in struggle', and as the masses responded an emotional Aref began to demand unity with the UAR and to refer to Iraq as a republic that is 'indivisible from the Arab nation'. Qasim and his allies began to panic and not simply for reasons of pure self-preservation. They were aware that an expansion of the UAR would be seen as a major threat to Israel and the shaky monarchy in Iran. Might not the West utilise genuine Kurdish fears of Arab hegemony and topple the regime? Aref's response to this was to argue that a united republic would make any such intervention in the present post-Suez climate unthinkable. In any case, Aflaq added, let the foreigners come. They will only suffer another blow and this time much worse than Suez.

Qasim and his communist allies were not prepared to move in the direction of the nationalists. Instead they decided to confront and defeat Aref and his supporters. The Ba'ath, unlike their communist rivals, simply did not have the popular support to foment a mass insurrection. Qasim was aware of this fact, but Aref was still intoxicated by the memory of the crowds who had flocked to him during his recent tour of the country.

On 11 September 1958, barely eight weeks since they had seized power, Aref was sacked as Deputy Commander-in-Chief of the Armed Forces. Two weeks later he was removed as Deputy Premier and Minister of the Interior, together with the Development Minister and Ba'athist leader Fuad al-Rikabi and the Nasserite Education Minister Jabir al-Umar. On 4 November, Aref was arrested and charged with 'having plotted against the safety of the motherland', in other words, treason. Aref had argued for a merger with the UAR and the nationalisation of the oil industry.[39] The fissiparousness that had plagued the House of Islam from the very beginning, and led to numerous defeats in Siqilliya, al-Andalus, and the Arab heartland, now began to wreck the nationalist edifice in the Arab East. None of this can be laid at the door of any Western imperialism or,

---

39 The Iraqi Communist Party uncritically backed Qasim at this time and was duly rewarded. Before Qasim removed Aref he moved the latter's Twentieth Infantry Brigade over a hundred miles outside Baghdad. The command of the Third Battalion (which Aref had led) was handed over to a couple of communist colonels. But the ICP supported Qasim for their own reasons. They were opposed to a union with Egypt and Syria. They were opposed to Nasser's 'neutralism' and wanted close ties with the USSR and China and this even led them, opportunistically, to defend Qasim when he delayed the nationalisation of the oil industry. They also attempted to build Qasim as a rival to Nasser, arguing foolishly that the Iraqi leader was the true 'pioneer of Arab nationalism'.

for that matter, Israel. It was a self-inflicted wound. The sectarian failure of communists and nationalists to reach a compromise became a tragedy for Iraq and the region as a whole. Israel's military victory in 1967 was only the most serious consequence.

Inside Iraq, the rift between Qasim and Aref seriously destabilised the functioning of the new republic. A polarisation began to take place inside the army. In March 1959, Aref's supporters stationed in army units in Mosul and Kirkuk and led by Brigadier Tabaqchali and Colonel Shawwaf (described as 'pan-Arab patriots' by Radio Cairo) attempted a coup, which was rapidly crushed by pro-Kassem troops backed by the communist irregulars of the People's Resistance Force. This led to a radio war. Radio Cairo incited Iraqis to overthrow 'the tyrant'; Radio Baghdad denounced 'foreign interference'. The President of the People's Court, Mahdawi, who had already sentenced Aref to death, added to the insult by announcing in open court that 'the Arab caravan is unaffected by barking dogs, even if some of them claim to be Arabs'.[40]

In October 1959, the nationalist response came in the form of an attempted assassination. A special unit of the Ba'ath, which included a 22-year-old party activist from Takrit named Saddam Hussein, carried out the action. Qasim was badly wounded, but survived. The coup that would have followed to replace him was foiled by a two-pronged operation carried out by the Communist Party. It mobilised public support on the streets, and its officers and soldiers in the army occupied the Ministry of Defence and established control of the crucial communications network. The communist leaders fondly imagined that Qasim would be grateful and they would strengthen their grip on the state apparatus. The exact opposite happened.

---

40 M. Perlmann, 'Nasser by the Rivers of Babylon', *Middle Eastern Affairs*, vol. 10, New York, April 1959, p. 154.

When he recovered, the Iraqi leader was astonished by the ease with which the communists had taken over the Ministry of Defence and carried out a purge of 'unreliable' officers. Qasim, contrary to what Nasser and the Ba'ath believed, was neither a secret communist nor remotely sympathetic to the Iraqi Communist Party. He was, in essence, an Iraqi nationalist – a reformer genuinely committed to alleviating poverty, but in political terms a social reformer rather than a radical. One of his complaints against Aref was that he was whipping up class hatred and unnecessarily alienating the people of property.[41] He wore the mask of an unassuming and reticent officer without any personal ambition. But this was contradicted by the manner in which the 1958 events had been manipulated. Qasim had insisted on keeping a majority of the Supreme Committee of the Free Officers uninformed as to what he and Aref were planning and when they would strike. This may have been mere caution but more likely it was a pre-emptive move to preserve the monopoly of power. These skills were brought into play after his success in removing Aref. Having utilised communist support to defeat the pan-Arabists, Qasim now turned on the Iraqi Communist Party. He organised a split amongst the top ranks and identified the splitters as the official party, but all this succeeded in doing was alienating the party's supporters (who remained loyal to their leaders) from the regime. He assumed that he would isolate the communists by pushing through his own policies, which he conceived as a 'third way' between socialism and capitalism. The fact that, unlike the

---

41 This aspect of Aref's politics was brought up at the trial to reassure the wealthy that all was under control. A major witness for the prosecution, Brigadier Abdi, testified thus:
    Witness: I sensed that some people, on hearing his speeches, took alarm. They imagined that no palaces and no other things signified the seizure of property.
    President of the Court: Did this affect the market?
    Witness: I believe it did.
Iraqi Defence Ministry Archives, cited in Batatu, op cit, p. 834.

From left to right: Communist Central Committee member Abdul-Karim Ahmad ad-Daud, Politbureau members Zaki Khairi, Baha-ud-Din Nuri and Muhammed Husain Abul-Iss, candidate member of Central Committee Abdul-Qadir Ismail, and Politbureau members Amer Abdallah and Jamal al-Haidar, leading the historic communist demonstration of over a half a million people on 1 May 1959.

men of the oligarchy, he was completely incorruptible on a personal level enhanced his prestige.

Today, in bad neo-liberal times, when any state regulation of the market is regarded as impermissible by the Empire's financial institutions, Qasim's socio-economic reforms make an impressive catalogue. They also help us to understand why there was genuine popular support for his regime. The changes of 1959-61 were focused on land reforms, which, like those in Egypt, restricted ownership of both irrigated and non-irrigated lands. The aim here was to strike at the power of rich, mainly absentee, landlords (56 percent of the land was owned by 3,000 landlords) and create a new middle class of peasant-proprietors in the countryside.

Urban reforms, too, were on their way. The rate of tax on the rich was raised from 40 percent to 60 percent on incomes above 20,000 dinars and this included rent from agricultural land. Death duties and inheritance taxes were also introduced to the country. Rent control was established in the cities and rents of rooms, apartments, and shops were reduced by 15–20 percent. Price control on essential commodities brought down the price of bread. Working hours were regulated. Industries employing over a hundred workers were legally obliged to build homes for them, and compulsory social insurance provisions were introduced for the first time. The slum-dwellers in Baghdad must have been amazed when they were informed that a new suburb was being built for them: ten thousand homes with electricity and water, new roads, schools, medical centres, and public baths. Not surprisingly this new district happily accepted the name assigned to it: the Revolution. This was later changed to Saddam City.

The existence and power of the Iraqi communists undoubtedly played an important role in the conceptualisation and implementation of these reforms. They rightly claimed the credit, but underestimated Qasim's

Abdul-Karim Qasim, chairman of the Supreme Committee of the Free Officers, 1956–58, and premier of Iraq, 1958–63. Son of a Sunni carpenter and a Shia-Kurdish mother, Qasim would proclaim 'I am Iraq.' A staunch Iraqi nationalist, he was executed after the Ba'athist coup of 1963.

capacity to use these measures to isolate and marginalise the communists. The manufacturing magnates in Iraq, too, understood the need for the changes and backed Qasim. They understood that it was the only way to prevent a communist revolution. In return Qasim imposed tough tariff barriers to aid the development of local industry. The contrast with the 'oligarchy of racketeers' could not have been more striking. And, what cannot be emphasised enough, millions of Iraqis regarded these changes as their due – human rights they had been denied for far too long. Some wanted to go further. Amongst these were the peasants who had discovered that many landlords were resisting land reforms, relying on legalities and bureaucratic support to delay or circumvent the handover of a large chunk of their estates to those who cultivated them. There were workers who complained that industrialists were delaying the implementation of the eight-hour day and bribing some of the state-sponsored trades unions to collaborate with them. It was the layer experiencing these difficulties that began to exert pressure on the Iraqi Communist Party from below. The communists and their numerous front organisations had grown phenomenally in the period after July 1958. The party's paper had a daily circulation of 30,000 (large for Iraq) and its supporters were to be found in every region and every institution of the country. Qasim, worried by this growth, attempted to ban 'narrow groupings and parties' in the name of revolutionary unity, just as his rival Nasser had done in Egypt. The communist response came the following day (1 May 1959) with a massive public demonstration dominated by two related slogans: 'Long Live the Leader Abd al-Karim Qasim' and 'Communists in the Government is a Mighty Demand.' Indeed it was – too mighty for Qasim to accept and one that created a real panic in Washington and London. The latter decided unilaterally to resume arms sales to Qasim in the hope of strengthening him against the communists. An emissary from Moscow arrived with an urgent instruction to the communists from

Nikita Khruschev not to destabilise the Qasim regime. Moscow felt that a communist victory in Baghdad would endanger its relations with Nasser and Arab nationalism.

The leaders of Iraqi communism were not immune to these pressures. Given their own political formation and history, this was hardly surprising, but at the same time the more astute amongst them realised that Qasim alone was incapable of resolving the situation.

Saint-Just's maxim ('Those who make the revolution halfway dig their own graves') now found a reflection in the Iraqi Politburo in the person of Husain ar-Radi, the Secretary of the Party, respected even by his fiercest opponents in other organisations for his integrity. Whatever their political weaknesses, it was difficult not to admire the courage of the communists. The general perception amongst ordinary people was that they were different from other politicians. They had actually sacrificed their lives for the poor. Their leader Fahd and two of his colleagues had been hanged in

Husain ar-Radi, first secretary of the Iraqi Communist Party 1955–63, tortured and killed after the Ba'ath coup of 1963. According to King Hussein of Jordan, names of many communists were provided to the Ba'ath by the CIA (see pp. 87–8 and footnote 42).

public by the oligarchy to demoralise, punish, and destroy their supporters, but they had survived and risen again with their prestige higher than ever before. Now they faced a serious test. Should they ditch Qasim and make a direct bid for state power? The question appeared simple enough, but hidden underneath were a layer of complex considerations. Was there a pre-revolutionary situation in Iraq? Might it not lead to a long and unwinnable civil war? What might be the international repercussions?

During the crucial Politburo meeting of May 1959, Husain ar-Radi argued in favour of defying Qasim's ultimatum and mobilising the party's support in a show of strength. He pointed out that mass consciousness was at its most radical and if their decision led to a test of strength they would win. A fully fledged revolution could succeed. But Moscow's instruction, conveyed by a returning member of the Iraqi Politburo, swung the balance in the direction of compromise. There was, however, a real problem. Since July 1958, the party had not been prepared ideologically for taking power and it had not primed the people for such a possibility by insisting on a set of demands and agitating continuously in their favour. If they had done so it is possible that they would have outflanked all their rivals. Instead, to stave off the challenge from Nasser and the nationalists, they promoted Qasim as 'the sole leader', their answer to Nasser, something that was simply not credible in the Arab world or even in Iraq, and even their most radical slogans had, at best, demanded that power be shared. Nothing more. In deference to Moscow, which was using Iraq as a bargaining counter in the Cold War, the Iraqi Communist Party delayed the nationalisation of the oil industry.

In these circumstances, to go for a complete rupture as suggested by ar-Radi was undoubtedly a risky strategy, but then every attempted revolution is a gamble, even in the best of circumstances. There is no automatic guarantee of success. The only serious question that needs to be posed is whether the conditions in the country favour taking such a risk. Was the festive energy of the crowds an accurate reflection of popular consciousness? If this was the case, and many believed it to be so, then Husain ar-Radi's instinct that it was time for a forward march was correct. But the Politburo in Baghdad deferred to the First Secretary in Moscow, isolated its own leader and decided to carry on in the same old way as before. They would not confront Qasim. His regime ran out of steam, its radical traits disappeared, it was paralysed by inertia and consequently became increasingly authoritarian over the next few years. At this point the communist leaders began to realise that their long association with and support of Qasim had demobilised some of their support. Qasim's decision to isolate the communists had given new heart to the landlords and barely a week passed without reports of peasants being attacked and killed for claiming their rights according to the law.

In 1963, the Ba'athists carried out a coup d'état and established an anti-Qasim and anti-communist coalition bringing Aref back to power. It was the end of Qasim and the Iraqi Communist Party. Qasim was tried and executed. The Iraqi Communist Party was vilified and persecuted; many of its leaders fled into exile while thousands of its members (especially in the army and air force) were hunted down, tortured, and killed. The Ba'athists who carried out the arrests and killings appeared to have lists of names and addresses. Where had they come from? The communists, naturally, saw an imperialist hand behind the vengeance. In Cold War times their view could easily be ignored, but King Hussein of Jordan, himself working closely with US intelligence agencies, confirmed communist suspicions. Meeting in the relaxed environment of the Hotel Crillon in Paris, the Jordanian ruler calmly informed Hasanein Heikal, a close personal friend of Nasser and, at that time, editor of Egypt's most influential daily, *al-Ahram*, of what had really taken place:

You tell me that American Intelligence was behind the 1957 events in Jordan. Permit me to tell you that I know for a certainty that what happened in Iraq on 8 February had the support of American Intelligence. Some of those who now rule in Baghdad do not know of this thing but I am aware of the truth. Numerous meetings were held between the Ba'ath party and American Intelligence, the more important in Kuwait. Do you know that on 8 February a secret radio beamed to Iraq was supplying the men who pulled the coup with the names and addresses of the Communists there so that they could be arrested and executed?[42]

The repression of Iraqi communists was systematic and brutal, prefiguring the massacres in Indonesia, which came two years later. What helped the party to survive was its strong support in the Kurdish areas of the country. Its martyred leader Fahd (as already noted, himself of Christian origin) had deliberately concentrated on building the party in regions where people were not simply dispossessed economically – this was the case throughout the country – but where their national, ethnic, and religious origins excluded them from being treated on their merits. He concentrated on recruiting Shia in the South, Kurds in the North, and Jews and Christians everywhere. The party's support for Kurdish aspirations won over thousands of Kurds. They survived the 1963 blood-Ba'ath better than their comrades on the Tigris or in the southern marshes, and many non-Kurdish communists survived with their help. Not, alas, Husain

---

42 Heikal published the interview in *al-Ahram*, Cairo, on 27 September 1963. It was never denied by any source. What has never been revealed is the list of names of the Ba'athist delegation that met the CIA in Kuwait. Did they include Saddam Hussein? The Ba'athist President, al-Baqr, himself later admitted that they had come to power 'using an American locomotive'. Yugoslav intelligence had also warned the Iraqi government that two of its ministers, Talib Shabeeb and Salah Jawad, were British agents. Given that the United States currently occupies Iraq, one hopes this is sufficient inducement to get the truth from the archives.

ar-Radi. He was captured, tortured, and executed. The scale of the disaster was horrendous and unleashed a bitter debate within the party. Four years later, in 1967, those of its leaders who had survived met in Prague to reassess the situation and some subjected themselves to fierce criticism:

> Our enemies and bourgeois friends frightened us with the possibility of civil war, a possibility for which, it is true, there were objective grounds; but had the civil war taken place at that time it would have in all probability turned in our favour and not in a dreadful slaughter of Communists and revolutionary democrats, as after 8 February 1963, when it actually broke out and reaction triumphed, having itself chosen the appropriate moment to set it off. Our shying from civil war in 1959, rather than securing us, made the disaster inevitable.... Had we seized the helm and without delay armed the people, carried out a radical agrarian reform ... granted to the Kurds their autonomy and, by revolutionary measures, transformed the army into a democratic force, our regime would have with extraordinary speed attained to the widest popularity and would have released great mass initiatives, enabling the millions to make their own history.[43]

They would never get another chance. The despair that gripped many of the party's militants led to further self-inflicted tragedies. One of those involved was a young Iraqi called Khalid Ahmed Zaki. And here, I must digress for a few pages to pay him homage.

When I first met Khalid, it was a few years after the anti-communist pogroms in Iraq. He was an exile in London, temporarily employed as a researcher by the Bertrand Russell Peace Foundation at its Shavers Place

---

43 'An Attempt to Appraise the Policy of the Communist Party of Iraq in the Period July 1958–1965', internal document.

Khalid Ahmed Zaki, Iraqi Marxist intellectual much influenced by Fidel Castro and Che Guevara. He organised an armed struggle in the southern marshes and was killed in action in 1968.

headquarters in the fashionable Piccadilly district of London. Shavers Place became a regular haunt for many third-world exiles. We would meet and exchange news and information about our respective dictatorships, and Bertrand Russell's secretary, Ralph Schoenman, would report regularly and optimistically on the state of the world revolution. The atmosphere was defiantly internationalist. The first time I saw him he was discussing the crisis in the Congo and the tragic fate of Patrice Lumumba. My own first encounter with street politics had been defying the military ban on all public assemblies and demonstrations and marching out on the streets of Lahore with a few hundred other students when news of Lumumba's murder had reached us in Pakistan in 1961. Now here was an Iraqi equally obsessed with the fate of the Congo. It cemented our comradeship.

It was Khalid Zaki who introduced me to the history of Iraqi communism. He talked of Fahd and the martyrs who had perished in the forties, of their executioner, Nuri al-Said, celebrated on the cover of *Time* magazine, of the events of 1958, and then we would return to the perennial subject – the failure of the party to make the revolution – and an unending discussion would follow. He was unsparing in his criticisms, and as I write this I can see him as he was then, a passionate revolutionary – the cliché applied to him ten times over. Nobility was written on his face. It was this as well as his integrity and steadfastness that drew people to him. None of this stopped him living life to the full. He could often be seen at parties in mid-sixties London, dancing vigorously while young women eyed him with undisguised interest and sometimes approached him with unrepressed ardour. He was active on that front as well.

One day he disappeared. There were rumours he had returned to Iraq to join the armed struggle against the dictatorship, but there was no concrete information. A year later in 1968, I heard he was dead, but nobody would talk of the circumstances. Nobody outside Iraq knew at the time. His comrades seemed to have disappeared as well. Thirty-seven years later, in 2003, I began to piece together the story of his ill-fated struggle and martyrdom. In late 1966 he had returned to Iraq where he joined the Baghdad section of the Iraqi Communist Party and immersed himself in the political life of the city. He gravitated towards the Intelligentsia Committee led by Najim Mahmood, a veteran party cadre fed up with the vacillations of the leadership. Mahmood provided Khalid with a detailed account of the divisions inside the leadership between two hardened factions, one completely loyal to Moscow, the other much more radical but also more confused. Mahmood and Zaki co-authored a stinging rebuke to the leadership. Signed by 'A group of the party cadre' the document denounced the politics and bureaucratic methods of both leadership factions; it demanded that the debate that was then taking place within the leadership should be made available to the entire membership, which should discuss and determine the future direction of the party. But this was not to be. Instead the party split and the Iraqi Communist Party (Central Command – Centcom) proposed a merger with the 'cadre group' led by Mahmood and Zaki. The latter joined the new Central Committee on condition that it approved the plans for launching an armed struggle against the dictatorship. This was agreed and funds were obtained by raiding a government paymaster in Sulaymaniyah.

The Popular Front For Armed Struggle consisted of Zaki and eleven other militants. The were inspired by the example of Che Guevara and now attempted to set up a base in the southern marshes of Iraq, site of the ancient slave revolt of the Zanj and a region where the Iraqi Communist Party had considerable support. Their plan was to launch a struggle that would trigger a national uprising. They captured a local police station in the region of Dawaya in Ghomogah Marsh, near Shatra in the Nasiriyah district. Their main base was near Majar al-Kabir (where six British soldiers, part of the occupying army, were shot dead in June 2003), lectured its inmates on the need to resist oppression and left with a new batch of weapons. When news of this reached Baghdad, the army over-reacted and despatched the Nineteenth brigade stationed in Diwaniyah to Nasiriyah to await orders. A sympathetic army officer alerted Najim Mahmood in Baghdad that troops were being sent in to quell the rebellion. He could not establish contact with the group. What he did not know was that the government knew the location of the guerrillas. A government helicopter was brought down and this led the army to overestimate the size of the force. They were surrounded. Realising this they attempted to break out. Five guerrillas from the region managed to escape. One (Amir al-Rikaby) was wounded and surrendered with the remaining five. Khalid Zaki was the only one killed in the cross-fire, brought down by a hail of machine-gun bullets. Though another source insists that two other militants – Shalash and Syed Duraan – also died. Najim Mahmood was arrested in Baghdad, charged with rebellion and brought before a military tribunal in Diwaniyah. The Iraqi President, Abdus Rehman Aref (the younger brother of Abdus Salam Aref, the previous president), had made it clear that he would not sign any death warrants in Baghdad. When Najim Mahmood faced the tribunal, the presiding colonel (from Mosul) said to him: 'I have never seen such poverty. You are right to teach them resistance.' The six captured guerrillas were sentenced to death and were to be executed in public in Nasiriyah on 30 July 1968. On 17 July, the Ba'ath organised a new coup and took power. The new President, Bakr, stopped all executions and after a few months ordered the release of all political prisoners. If Khalid had survived, he might still have been alive.

The inner wounds had still not healed when I met one of the survivors on the Left Bank in June 2003. Paris on a beautiful summer day evokes enough local memories and Amir al-Rikaby did not want to discuss the southern marshes, though we did briefly discuss Khalid. I had wanted to know everything. What had they said to each other as they realised they were surrounded? Had Khalid made a speech before the encounter? But Amir did not want to relive the episode. Only once, when I asked if the decision to launch the armed struggle had been taken by Khalid alone, did he reply. 'No. Everyone voted for it.' And then I stopped asking questions about the past.

We spoke of the present occupation and his face suddenly cleared. He expressed total confidence that the resistance could only grow. 'Collaboration was a filthy option. This was the instinct of most Iraqis, no matter how much they despised Saddam Hussein or had suffered during the Ba'athist period.' And this was one of them speaking to me. For the quislings he felt only contempt, and he was entertained by the rapid return of Ahmed Chalabi and his sidekicks to the imperial motherland to get new orders before they returned. But Amir was also angry that the rest of the world had fallen into line so quickly, accepted the occupation and, as always, left the Iraqis to their fate. He was depressed that the antiwar movement had virtually disappeared, arguing that 'their behaviour is tainted with traditional prejudices against the South'. Of course there were many exceptions, and here the name of Noam Chomsky came up.[44]

---

44 What his detractors in the US media do not realise is that the main reason for Chomsky's enormous popularity and prestige in Asia and Latin America is not that he offers strategic or

A few days later I was discussing the Paris encounter on the phone with an old Iraqi friend, Faris Wahhab. A socialist during his student days, Faris had left the Ba'ath party together with other dissidents and joined an independent Marxist group. He, too, had turned up in London as a stateless exile, but in the early seventies. He was helping edit an Arabic magazine, *Arab Revolution*, and that was when I first met him. Later he was compelled to leave Britain and we lost contact with each other. He went to Algeria. Subsequently he was forced to seek exile in the Far East. It was Faris who informed me that Amir al-Rikaby was one of the heroes of Haidar Haidar's novel *The Banquet of Seaweed*.[45] Set in the east Algerian city of Anabe (Bonne) during the late seventies, the novel is a reflection on Arab politics and the defeat in Iraq. The two principal characters in the novel – Mehdi Jawad and Mihyar al-Bahilly – are both Iraqi communist exiles. Mihyar is a fictional portrait of Rikaby. The trauma they have suffered has affected them in different ways. Mehdi, who has been there longer, has now realised that Algiers is not unlike Baghdad: 'The city is beautiful, surrounded with forests and sea, but like any Arab city it is dreary, ruled by tyranny, hunger, bribery, corruption, religion, hatred, ignorance, cruelty and murder.' Mihyar is still hopeful that the Algerian masses will

---

tactical advice (which he does not), but that he speaks a truth that is uncomfortable to those in power. In the world of today this is a rarity.

45   This novel by a Syrian writer – *Walimah li-A'shab al-Bahr*, Damascus, 1998 (6th reprint) – was written over twenty years ago and recently (2000) was reprinted as a classic by the Ministry of Culture in Egypt. Its republication provoked an outcry from Islamists, who claimed there were blasphemous passages, etc. The novel was withdrawn. Sabry Hafez produced an excellent essay on this incident for the *New Left Review*, 'The Novel, Politics and Islam' (*NLR* 5, September/October 2000), which was widely translated and discussed. Far from being blasphemous in any sense this was a powerful historical novel, 'a broad panorama of the failure of the Arab revolution, complex in structure and epic in scope'. I had no idea at the time this was published that the novel contained references to Khalid Zaki or that a central character was based on Amir al-Rikaby. The English translation of the passages quoted is by Faris Wahhab, who wants me to inform the reader that he is not a professional translator. This is a statement of fact.

move forward again. His vibrancy leads to a long dialogue between the two men on revolution: one crushed in Iraq and the other triumphant in Algeria. Both men have been physically defeated, but their disagreements reveal that their spirit has not been destroyed. And in this novel I discovered elements of the story that Amir al-Rikaby had not wanted to discuss on that beautiful June day in Paris.

A few pages into the novel (p. 19), the two exiles stumble across each other:

As they saw each other, Mihyar al-Bahilly began to shout excitedly.

'What the devil … is that really you? Here? No one told me. Which devil-inspired stars brought you to this corner of the globe?'

The two men hugged each other. It was a celebratory hug, filled with joy and relief. After the warm embrace, a silence. Then Mehdi Jawad spoke.

'We meet again at last. This time to inject a Marxist note into the Maghreb. You take care of the Ideology and Philosophy and I'll take the Language.'

Inside the café, Mihyar was elated. The location thrilled him. He sits sipping his coffee as he smokes, his eyes shine with a sharp light. He speaks:

'We are now in the sacred land, the land where the Arabs surprised themselves with a revolution. Oh man, the revolution of the million martyrs. When I landed from the plane I went on my knees to kiss the soil.'

'Your political temperature hasn't returned to normal, Mihyar,' said Mehdi. 'Tell me something. As you kissed the earth were you sure the blood did not smell completely rotten?'

'Stop this cynicism,' replied Mihyar. 'One day soon we shall visit the graves of the revolutionaries and all the places where the battles were fought. I tell you the Algeria of the Revolution is like a luminous beacon in the darkness of Arab humiliation. I am as happy as a child who meets his mother after a long absence. Imagine! I am in the heart of the memories of this revolution. First, I was appointed to teach at the Institute of the Children of the Martyrs. Second, I found lodging in the house of a widow who lived with the revolutionaries in the mountains. She was with Taher Al-Zubairi himself.'

Mehdi Jawad interrupted his friend sarcastically, 'And thirdly, in order to complete your revolutionary purity, I think you should marry this revolutionary widow and achieve your dream of revolutionary unity with her.'

Questions began to explode from Mihyar. What is the situation of the Iraqis here, Arab missions, Algerian society, culture ...? He did not wait for Mehdi to reply. Occasionally he replied himself: he explained the conflict inside the revolution and the power struggle that eliminated Ben Bella, he gestured in admiration of this fallen, betrayed revolutionary: 'Ben Bella is the father of socialism, I saw in him the Arab Castro, I felt he was moving towards Marxism. This Boumedienne cannot be trusted, a military man, isolationist, an Islamic head and African feathers, but his heart is Algerian. Occasionally he wears Arabic customs, I am of course talking about the authority, but the people here make miracles ...'

'You are still infected by the rays of the Saints. I worry that you will burn yourself out.'

'We have to be like this in these times.'

'But why tackle all the questions at once. There is plenty of time to clarify our ideas. The Revolution and the people here are more complex than you imagine. People are different when in battle and after the battle. Slow down a bit, little brother.'

'We should find a way to contact the revolutionaries. I know the banned Altaliaa [CP] Party is operating underground.'

Mehdi Jawad was patient.

'Your intentions are noble and your head is filled with memories, but after you have been here for a while, you will understand what Albert Camus meant when he said, "With them I am a stranger and to get rid of this alienation I go and stare at the sea."'

'No,' said Mihyar. 'It it is not like that. Camus was neutral, alienated because he was French.'

'But those you dream about have been turned to stone. Terror did that. People here have become as mute as a granite mountain. Later you will detect this terror on their faces. I know. I tried before you came to break through this granite. It is impossible.'

'Why?'

'Suspicious. They do not trust anybody after their ordeals; the revolution has entered its menopausal stage. Your imaginary comrades are in Europe and Paris now.'

'Europe? What the hell are they doing there?'

'It seems they have moved their revolutionary project to Paris. They have set up some sort of "Exiles association" similar to nineteenth-century communists after the failure of the German revolution and the victory of Bismark.'

'Strange! But the battle is here.'

When he uttered the sentence, 'But the battle is here,' he seemed disturbed. His face was like a cloudy sky. He lit a new cigarette from the old one, ordered another black coffee and sighed. Mehdi Jawad wanted to tell him that in the age of exile the sun rises from the east and the west, but before he could say anything Mihyar frowned and announced, 'Oh what a sad age!'

This was a man infected by the craze of revolutionary wars, an intellectual still thrilled by Blanqui, the glory of the Commune, the raid on Santa Clara and the Arms, the Arms – who ever had them would have God's word on earth. A small band of brave men will set history on its feet, and thus began Mohammad then Ali bin Mohammad in the vicinity of Basrah and then Abu Taher Al-Qurmati, and Che Guevara and then Mihyar Al-Bahilly. He was from Basrah from a mid-Euphrates religious dynasty and the old Bahillys and the Imam Hussain bin Ali – the dynasty that carried its blood in their hands with its white coffins on its body and walked to its fate with death its only victory.

When he waged the armed struggle with Khalid Ahmed Zaki and the doomed guerrilla war in the marshes, he was under the illusion that he was continuing the heritage of bloody martyrdom, perpetuated in the many passion plays that are performed in the morning or evening. This was the scream from the past to break out anew in the twentieth, thirtieth or the fiftieth centuries, breaking all the walls of the age of despotism, hunger, mass genocides for the benefit of people beaten and humiliated and buried under the beastly authority of the Caliphs, princes, dummy generals, and the parties that capitulated.

Later in the novel (p. 133) there is a moving description of Khalid Zaki, who makes an appearance in the novel under his own name. Amir al-Rikaby must have talked at length with the novelist, when the tragedy was still strong in him and he needed to talk as one does after the death of a loved one or the break-up of a relationship or some other emotional trauma. And the novelist captured the moment. He recorded it in his own way, with his own nuances, but I recognised the portrait of the man I had met so often in Shavers Place.

Ever since he [Khalid Ahmed Zaki] entered Iraq secretly from London, where he was a member of the Bertrand Russell Foundation, the Rightist leadership [of the ICP] was nervous of this adventurist, a

Guevarist infected with the ideas of the European new left and the excitements of the Tupamaros and the guerrilla wars of Latin America.

A gentle, sweet, and splendid human being. When you see him for the first time, he could easily be a romantic prince from old Wales or medieval Spain. When he grins, he blushes in a feminine way leaving a large rosy patch on his pristine white cheeks.

What brought this man from the foggy streets of London to this strange time in Iraq? Mihyar Al-Bahilly is asking himself all this, but as he stares at the childlike face, he sees its other side and realises how often the appearance hides the reality. During his acquaintance with him he did not study as carefully as he should have the fine details behind the smooth white skin.

In the heart of the Middle Euphrates, and while crossing the Marshes, enduring the mud, the fatigue, and the beats of terror, Mihyar al-Bahilly will realise what brought this gentle romantic to banish caution and come to the lone kingdom of death.

He will hold the body in his arms, a body pierced with bullets, its blood clots mixed with mud, and he will call on him to rise again. Deep inside Mihyar's soul there is a sorrow for the words that sprang out from him when he disagreed with Khalid, accusing him of retreating and saying that he was against suicidal death.

Khalid Ahmed Zaki, with the awareness of a revolutionary who lived through the hollow experience of the peaceful democratic line that brought catastrophe to the party, he would present his theoretical document which emphasises the replacement of a political circus by an armed struggle, starting from the marshes. He would call on the political leadership to be the vanguard of this struggle. He would then go on to define an action plan that relied on the countryside without neglecting the cities, pointing out the necessity of unifying all other progressive sectors.

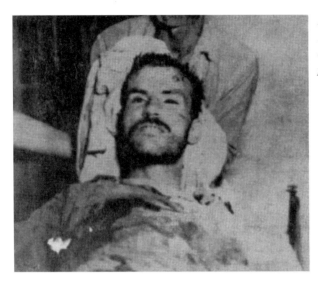

Khalid Ahmed Zaki's dead body being displayed to the press in 1968.

I began to understand Amir al-Rikaby. Perhaps, there are some things in life too painful to be recorded by history and which are best left to fiction, which can sometimes be more honest than history. The encounter in the southern marshes during which Khalid Ahmed Zaki lost his life in 1968 barely rates a footnote in the numerous books on Iraq. Why should it? It was only one death amongst many. No blame attaches to the historians. But it was different for us who knew and cherished him. We recognised that something terrible had happened. The loss was incomparable. His intellectual capacities, practical abilities, and human qualities were much needed in the decades that followed and even more so today. It was an awful tragedy, a life prematurely truncated, a departure that symbolised the defeat of an entire generation. Mudhaffar al-Nawab's latest poem is incomprehensible outside this context.[46]

---

46   See Chapter 2, pp. 38–39.

The radical colonels and communists and independent armed factions, and Maoism and Guevarism, and everything else – the entire shipload had sunk to the bottom. And now, rejoicing in its downfall, were the old enemies, the cutthroats of the Ba'ath, their hands already coated with the blood of their opponents. They were preparing to do what the communists had shrunk from when the moment was ripe – to seize power and this time on their own.

5

BA'ATHISM: SADDAM AND GUMHURRIYA*

And the poets fled, no longer able to think or sing in the midst of the horror. And the years passed, but memories of torture and death continued to haunt Iraqis at home or in exile. And they often asked themselves whether what had happened was inevitable and, occasionally, this was followed by another question, even more relevant. Would it have been any different if the communists had come to power instead? Would Aziz al-Hajj have made a more benevolent dictator than Saddam? After all, the origins of the Ba'ath were not so different from those of other secular political groupings. Many of the young members they recruited in the forties and fifties shared the same radical anti-imperialist stance and were of a similar class composition to those drawn to other species of nationalism, socialism, or communism. None of these other movements were, in any case, very large.

The failure of liberal and social-democratic parties in the imperial heart-lands of Europe to demand freedom for the colonies and the protectorates played a big part in alienating educated young Arabs from the traditions of these organisations. The remaining models in the first third of the twentieth century were fascism and communism. Some nationalists were attracted to

---

* The word 'gumhurriya' is used as a synonym for the republic and/or democracy in the Muslim world.

the German model. What appealed were its nationalism and its obvious strength, capable of defeating the British and French Empires. What they ignored was the openly expressed desire of German imperialism to build its own Empire. This attraction, however, was considerably reduced after the two decisive Soviet victories of the Second World War at Stalingrad and Kursk. The Red Army's offensive that ended in Berlin had a global impact, leading to a dramatic increase in the size of communist parties everywhere.

The small group of Syrian intellectuals who founded the Ba'ath 'Renaissance' in the forties had never been attracted to fascism. Its most influential thinker and founder, Michel Aflaq, had studied in France and was initially attracted to the French Communist Party. The refusal of the latter — during the Popular Front government of 1936 — to insist on colonial freedom as part of the Popular Front's programme surprised and alienated Aflaq. It was this experience that led him to assume that communist party leaders would always place their own narrow interests or those of the Soviet state before the objective needs of the poor and the oppressed, especially in the colonies. If this was a demonstration of 'proletarian internationalism' in practice, then it might be better for people living in the colonial or semi-colonial world to forget high-sounding phrases, forget the Soviet Union, and struggle for self-emancipation as simple nationalists.[47] This is how Aflaq reasoned when he and Salah Bitar decided to found a new party in 1943. And this view became a dogma after 1948, when the Arab Communist parties, with the exception of Iraq (while Fahd was alive), backed the formation of Israel simply because that was official Soviet policy at the time. They did so, and this is worth repeating, in the face of

---

47 'During this period' — Aflaq was referring to the mid-thirties in Paris — 'I admired the hardness of the Communists' struggle against the French. I used to admire the toughness of the young men in the Communist Party. After 1936 and the assumption of power in France by the Leon Blum Front government, I became disenchanted and felt betrayed.' A useful account of the formation and early period of the Ba'ath is contained in Kamel S. Abu Jabar, *The Arab Ba'ath Socialist Party*, New York, 1966.

stiff opposition from many Jewish members of the Egyptian and Iraqi parties. One of the founders of the Egyptian Communist Party changed his Jewish name in protest against the creation of Israel and refused to leave his country.[48] But none of this could excuse the official position adopted by these parties. It became an important element in the deep-rooted hostility between the two anti-imperialist currents in the region, making it much easier for the Ba'ath to become a mass party.

In the fifties, before it became a party of power in Iraq and Syria, and for a brief period afterwards, there were open debates and arguments inside the party that were usually resolved by ballots. The bullets were a later innovation. The historic founders of the party, Michel Aflaq and Salah Bitar, were men of moderate temperament; both were teachers by profession and had studied together at the Sorbonne a decade after the First World War. They often conveyed the impression of two cultured European socialists trapped in the murky maze of the Arab political bazaar and, to their great distaste, forced to haggle. While it is true that, once his party came to power, Aflaq was incorruptible on a personal level, he was not immune to using his position as the founder in order to get his way on even the most trivial issues. It was bad enough negotiating with Nasser and the Syrian communists, but when the factional struggles erupted inside the Ba'ath, its founders were horrified. Aflaq, despite his ideological hostility to communism, was not in favour of massacring its supporters as the Iraqi Ba'athists had done after the 1963 coup in Baghdad. The fact that the Ba'athi primitives in Iraq, who were – to the delight of Fort Langley – organising the tortures and executions of their opponents, were also critical of Aflaq and his supporters and denounced them for being in

---

48   When I was last in Cairo in 2002, he was in his nineties, still intellectually alert, proud of his past and his library. Events, he informed all visitors, had vindicated his opposition to Zionism and much else.

the grip of 'bourgeois idealism' confirmed the party's founder in all his prejudices against leftist extremism.

At the Sixth National Congress held in Damascus from 5 to 23 October 1963, the 'radical factions' of the Iraqi and Syrian groups united and obtained a majority. This was fairly normal behaviour for a political party. They had clearly prepared for this and had won over some of the key delegations. As a result all their resolutions were carried. To the utter astonishment of the two old Sorbonne graduates, the congress declared itself in favour of 'socialist planning', 'collective farms run by elected peasants committees', and 'democratic workers' control of the means of production'; naturally, this meant basing the party on 'workers and peasants'. (The congress thereby prefigured the demands of the 1968 Sorbonne 'soviet'.) Just in case there was any doubt as to who they had in their sights, the congress rejected the growth and position of 'ideological notability' inside the party. Aflaq was enraged, declaring at the end of the congress that 'this party is no longer my party'. This really delighted his opponents since that was exactly what they wanted to hear. Fearing for their own safety, the 'ideological notables' retreated to their tents to discuss the debacle. They would now prepare to raise the inner-party struggle to a new pitch.

The Sixth Congress, in reality, was an oblique tribute to the Iraqi Communist Party. The Ba'ath leaders engaged in working with trades unions and peasant organisations had realised that the only serious way to displace the communists was by stealing their ideas and implementing them. Killing communists was not the solution, especially as the executions had angered not only Aflaq but many rank-and-file Ba'athists. The Damascene conversion of the Sixth Congress to Marxist rhetoric, however, had gone some way beyond the programme of Arab communism.[49] Ali Saleh as-

---

49 Some of the language, especially 'democratic workers' control of the means of production' and a 'workers' and peasants' government', could have been lifted straight out of Leon Trotsky's

Saadi – the Secretary of the Iraqi party – and his supporters had, at least on paper, positioned the Ba'ath to the left of the Arab communist parties.[50] Aflaq was livid. Later, he would provide his own account of the Sixth Congress:

> the manner of proceeding was alien to the Party … the forming of blocs, the professional exploitation of the party's Rules … and verbal quibble and sophistry. It doesn't make sense that Ba'athists should turn into men of this sort when they hold in their hands the fate of millions … and when the whole nation is waiting to see whether the Ba'athi experiment is worthy of life. … Let us speak plainly. On what basis have you risen to leadership? Is it to smooth the path for so-and-so, who only a year ago had been a member of the Communist party, to conspire against our principles? With feelings of love I cautioned the members of the National Congress, but in vain. I told them: 'I have become of the past. I have no longer any worldly ambition. I put my life in this party and desire nothing other than to see it grow and truly prosper. This is why I am filled with anxiety …'. I told them to question me and not prevent me from speaking, for things got to such a point at the Congress that once I asked for the floor and was turned down …[51]

'Transitional Programme'. This did make me wonder whether a few Trotskyists had 'entered' and impregnated the Ba'ath. Some of the radical Ba'athists who subsequently left and established far-left magazines in Beirut and London, like my old friend Fawaz Trabulsi, were not unacquainted with Trotsky's ideas, but they were nowhere near the positions of command, even though their ideas reached the top.

50   The distinguished novelist Abderrahman Munif was for two critical years (1960–62) a member of the Ba'ath National Command – the highest authority of the party between congresses. He constantly annoyed the hierarchy by refusing to wear the regulation suit and tie, and a year after Saddam Hussein became head of state, Munif left Baghdad. One assumes it was too painful an experience to record in fiction.

51   'The First Utterance of Comrade Michel Aflaq', Arab Ba'ath Socialist Party, quoted extensively in Batatu, op cit, pp. 1021–2.

But the love disappeared rapidly and Aflaq made a fateful decision. He mobilised the military Ba'athists to overturn the decisions and the elected leadership of the Party Congress.[52] In November 1963, the Iraqi Ba'ath was in session at an Extraordinary Congress convened to discuss the implementation of the decisions made at the Sixth Party Congress. These decisions had clearly embarrassed the Ba'ath ministers in the military government. Symbolically, it was just as a new leadership was being elected that fifteen armed military officers entered the conference hall. Their agitated leader, Colonel al-Mahdawi, commander of the Third Tank Regiment, pointed his machine-gun at Saleh as-Saadi and informed the delegates: 'I have been told by Comrade Michel Aflaq, the philosopher of the party, that a gang lords over the party in Iraq and has its analogue in Syria, and that the two had laid their heads together and dominated the Sixth National Congress, therefore they must be eliminated.'[53]

With guns pointing at them, the delegates did as they were told and 'elected' the pro-Aflaq Ba'athis, who thus obtained a majority. Saleh as-Saadi and other majority leaders were arrested, taken to the airport and put on a military plane bound for Madrid. As news of what had happened spread to the party's branches in Baghdad, riots broke out. Barricades were set up and the demonstrators occupied key sectors of the city, including Broadcasting House and the telephone exchange. Two Ba'ath pilots managed to evade security and once their bomber jets were airborne, they

---

52 Here the contrast with the communists was very clear. While military leaders often held senior positions in the communist parties in the Soviet Union (Zhukov), China (Lin Piao), Vietnam (Vo Nguyen Giap), in Iraq there was a very clear division between the Ba'ath Party and the army. Politics was in command. The party leadership made all key decisions. This is also the case in Cuba where, despite the fact that a guerrilla army made the revolution, a political party took over. A similar model was imposed on the satellite states of Eastern Europe where, with the brief exception of Poland, politics was conducted by the ruling party. The Arab east was different in this regard.
53 Batatu, op cit.

Pre-Saddam Hussein Ba'ath leaders, who rebelled against Michel Aflaq. They were later executed on Saddam's orders.

threatened a civil war unless the Ba'ath leadership was reinstated: they attacked the air base and fired warning rockets in the direction of the Presidential Palace. Given that the Ba'ath was part of an anti-communist coalition government and did not have full control of the state apparatus, this was an astonishing development. A political struggle inside the party had moved to the streets of Baghdad.

By noon most of the city was in the hands of the rebels. The Ba'athist Prime Minister, understandably, refused to let the army restore order. It would have meant destroying his own base of support. To avoid a full-scale civil war between the two factions, Michel Aflaq, accompanied by the Syrian President (also a Ba'athist), flew in from Damascus and attempted to stitch together a compromise. This failed. The Iraqi President, Abdus Salam Aref, used the internal battles of the Ba'ath to assume complete power. He ordered the army and air force to end the rebellion: by the time the sun had set on that same day it was all over. The following morning, Aref removed his turbulent partners from the government. The Ba'ath had suffered a heavy blow.

More important than the setback itself was the decision taken by the 'ideological notables' to militarise the party. Having used a small group of army officers to override the will of the majority, Aflaq effectively sanctioned a military dictatorship inside the party. The end of all pretensions to inner-party democracy led inexorably to the military control of the state. The examples of both Syria and Iraq are instructive in this regard. From being a party committed to an Arab renaissance, the Ba'ath, incapable of resolving the rift between the two states it controlled, degenerated into a bureaucratic clique of power-hungry officers, increasingly buttressed by repression and dependent on tribal and clan loyalties. Saddam Hussein and Hafez Asad did not create this system, but became its most creative beneficiaries. By instituting personal dynasties, the twin dictators encouraged a further degeneration. Self-preservation became the single most important principle guiding the Iraqi and Syrian regimes from the seventies onwards. The unity of the Arab nation still existed on the level of ideology, but in practice the local state had become the only pillar of the Ba'athist regimes. In November 1970, Asad's military faction removed the Ba'ath politicians and took direct control of Syria. Michel Aflaq fled to Baghdad.

In both Syria and Iraq the Military Committees of the Ba'ath became the real controllers of the party; the other dominant institution was the Mukhabarat: the security and intelligence service.[54] The Iraqi leadership

---

54 At a conference in Beirut in 1997, a Palestinian friend who had been exiled in Damascus for thirty years told me how a few of the most gifted, if totally cynical, leftist intellectuals in Syria had joined the secret police. When he upbraided one of them (an especially talented essayist and ex-Althusserian who had studied at the *Ecole Normale Superior* in the seventies) the apostate replied: 'At least in this office nobody can spy on us! We can read what we want, see the latest videos, write poetry, enjoy life and do what we can to stop people like you from being locked up. It's much better than becoming prostitutes like most of the French intellectuals. I mean, look at Bernard Henri-Levy.' Whenever my friend returned from abroad, two of the old sixties intellectuals-turned-cops would come to see him and borrow the latest Derrida, Debray, and Baudrillard he had brought back from Paris. 'Whatever else,' he told me, 'this is probably the best-educated secret police cadre in the world.'

was not happy and Saddam Hussein voiced their concern in public after the Syrian coup:

> Our relations with Syria are good but, as far as the Syrian Ba'ath Party is concerned, the case is different. None of the crises this party went through after 1963 revealed a change in its mentality. As to us, we refuse to admit that tanks, guns or fighter planes can replace normal party methods.[55]

The collective memory of the Iraqi Ba'ath has always been notoriously selective.

The Sixth Party Congress, whatever one's view of the decisions reached, had united a majority of Iraqi and Syrian Ba'athists on the basis of a common political programme. Michel Aflaq had decided to use military force to crush the majority. This led to the virtual collapse of the party in Iraq and exacerbated factionalism within its ranks. Aflaq then took charge and appointed the new leadership: Hasan al-Bakr headed the key Military Committee and his cousin Saddam Hussein was made Secretary-General of the party. This pair began the task of reorganisation. When a vacuum emerged within the army after the Iraqi President Abdus Salam Aref died in a plane crash in 1966, it took two years of careful planning for al-Bakr and Saddam Hussein to seize power via the military. There were no spontaneous mass mobilisations.

Asad did the same in Syria, though in his case it was a much nastier operation, as he had to remove a radical Ba'athist government from power and reverse most of its economic decisions.[56] Aflaq, happy to use the army

---

55 Interview with the Beirut daily *L'Orient–Le Jour*, 18 May 1971, cited in Eberhard Kienle, *Ba'ath versus Ba'ath: the Conflict Between Syria and Iraq 1968–1989*, London and New York, 1990.
56 In Damascus, after the 1967 war, I met Dr Youssif Zouyyain, the Syrian Prime Minister,

in Iraq to get his way, was not pleased by developments in Syria. He felt that once the radicals were removed, his moderate supporters should be reinstated and Salah Bitar be returned to office in a high capacity. The very thought enraged Asad and his anger was conveyed to the 'ideological notables' who left hurriedly for Baghdad. In their absence the two key founders of the party were tried for treason and sentenced to death. Years later Asad commuted the sentence, but when faced with a series of rebellions at home he made sure that there was no alternative: in 1980 Salah Bitar was assassinated in Paris.[57]

Regionalism and factionalism dominated relations between the two parties; narrow state interests determined relations between the two states. Saddam Hussein and Hafez al-Asad shared the same political universe. Both had defeated their respective radicals; both had revived the fortunes of middle-class traders and shopkeepers; both had created a structure where each leader sat at the top of a political pyramid designed to give

---

and other Ba'ath leaders. Zouyyain was confident that Syria would become the 'Cuba of the Middle East', but their optimism was not infectious. There is a brief account of this meeting in my *Clash of Fundamentalisms*, London and New York, 2003, pp. 123–4. Soon after the appearance of the book, an elderly Arab couple stopped me on a London street. They were friends of Zouyyain. He had heard I had written about him and wanted to see my book. Would I oblige? Naturally, I agreed to despatch a copy. But where was he living these days? 'In Budapest,' came the reply. I assumed that after Asad's 1970 coup, Zouyyain had been granted exile by the Hungarian regime. How many radical third-world exiles were there still in Russia and Eastern Europe? Had they readjusted? Zouyyain was an Edinburgh-trained doctor of medicine, but there were many others. Had they all become businessmen?

57 The most thorough account of inter-Ba'ath and inter-state rivalry between Iraq and Syria is contained in Kienle's meticulous study *Ba'ath versus Ba'ath*. Kienle's thesis was amply vindicated the year his book was published by the Syrian decision to become part of the US-sponsored coalition during the First Gulf War. Asad's son, Bashar, who succeeded his father to the Ba'athi throne in Damascus, was much more circumspect during the Second Gulf War of 2003. He was the only Arab leader to publicly declare that he hoped that the United States and Britain would be defeated. This probably had much more to do with self-preservation than Ba'athist solidarity or Arab unity, but was refreshing nonetheless. For the current situation see Charles Glass, 'Is Syria Next?', *London Review of Books*, 24 July 2003.

each despot total power; and both used an anti-imperialist rhetoric in public while fondling the United States in private. And neither was a novice when it came to repression. Saddam destroyed the communists and crushed the Kurds; his Syrian co-thinker ordered the deaths of ten thousand people in Hamah – Islamists and secular oppositionists who had risen against the regime. But they behaved like rival Mafia barons, concerned only with maintaining their personal power. Politically they were brothers, but as the Italians say, '*fratelli, coltelli*' – where there are brothers, there are knives.[58] This is not what the Sorbonne-educated notables had in mind when they founded the party but this is where they had led it.[59]

And if these two Ba'ath leaders proved incapable of uniting Iraq and Syria when both were under Ba'athist rule, were their rhetoric in favour of Arab unity and their semi-mystical references to 'the Arab' even remotely credible? In fact, most of the post-Ottoman states that emerged

---

58 Cited in 'To Kill a Chinese Mandarin' by Carlo Ginsburg, in his *Wooden Eyes: Nine Reflections on Distance*, London, 2002.

59 The Palestinian Arab scholar Hanna Batatu later wrote a twin volume on Syria, published a year before his death in 2000. It is a stunning work, replete with brilliant insights, painstakingly objective and meticulously researched. Apart from providing a history of the peasantry and its religious beliefs, Batatu's account of the early Syrian Ba'ath and the Asad dictatorship, based partially on interviews with participants and eyewitnesses, makes it an indispensable work. Writing in the nineties, Batatu permitted himself the odd digression. My favourite is a section in Chapter 16 headed, 'A Few Preliminary General Observations on "Democratic" Rhetoric and the Realities of Life'. Here Batatu argues that 'Hafiz al-Asad and American politicians have one thing in common: their "democratic" rhetorical flourishes. In their public pronouncements they romanticize the power of the people, but in their actions the citizens at large seldom constitute a crucial driving force, except in moments of crisis or in times of unrest or rising popular consciousness.' While underlining the differences, he poses an important question: '… how meaningful is the role of the majority of the people in the determination of public affairs in a country like the United States in the context of a political landscape occupied by huge corporations, massive state and military complexes, and big units for the moulding and manipulation of opinion.' Hanna Batatu, *Syria's Peasantry, the Descendants of Its Lesser Rural Notables and Their Politics*, Princeton, 1999, pp. 204–7.

after the First World War had slowly begun to develop their own identities and their own ruling elites. There were two interrelated reasons for the persistence of an Arab nationalism: oil and Israel. It was neither sentimentality nor guilt for the Judeocide, or the effectiveness of a pro-Israel lobby, nor the biased reportage of the *New York Times* that necessitated the buttressing of Israel as the Prussia of the Arab East. It was oil. And it was oil that compelled Washington to spend billions in order to shore up the 'security of the region' via Israel, the Saudi monarchy, and the British-created Gulf states.[60] It is this reality that produced the triune evil against which nationalists of every hue were pledged to battle: US imperialism, Zionism, and Arab reaction. They did not do this very effectively and were, for the most, partly engaged in fighting each other.

In Iraq, however, the Ba'ath had important concerns other than fratricide. A serious domestic rival existed in the shape of the Iraqi Communist Party and despite the brutalities inflicted on it and the casualties it sustained, this organisation had survived in clandestinity. Its Kurdish strongholds had remained virtually unaffected. It had a functioning underground leadership in Baghdad, while another leadership met regularly in the more relaxed environment of baroque Prague.

The defeat of 1963 had created a serious divide inside the party. Over the next four years its orthodoxies were challenged from within. This was in keeping with the changing times. Moscow's monopoly had been broken. The Second Declaration of Havana, the continuing resistance of the Vietnamese, and the early period of the Sino-Soviet split had generated a storm that broke down the shutters of world communism and swept through its portals. The dust had not settled when a leading faction of the

---

60 These statelets have today become the most expensive imperial petrol stations in the world, run by eccentric franchise-holders whose passions now include competing architecturally with Chicago and Shanghai, despite an infrastructure largely dependent on migrants.

General Ahmad Hasan al-Bakr (left), President of Iraq and Secretary-General of the Iraqi Ba'ath from 1968 to 1979, with Michel Aflaq, founder of the Ba'ath Party.

Iraqi Communist Party decided it wanted to revenge the past and the only way forward lay through launching an armed struggle against the dictatorship. It argued for a complete break with the past practices of the party, including its over-reliance on Moscow and subordination to its needs. It was argued that if the communists did not take the initiative now, they would be outmanoeuvred and outflanked by the Ba'ath as they were in 1963. What was being proposed was also the best possible means of self-defence against what lay ahead. The argument was far from foolish, but it was premature. But they were heady days and the party became split. The Central Command faction began to make immediate preparations for an exemplary armed struggle on the Cuban model and was expelled from the party at a special conference in 1967.

The Central Command plan was to launch a resistance movement in the southern marshes, where the party did have considerable support, and create a liberated zone. From here they would move northwards and, later, armed Kurdish communists and nationalists would move southwards; both columns would meet in Baghdad, which would be virtually liberated by then by an uprising of the poor. It was all planned with the purest of motives, but it assumed a rising level of mass consciousness that, alas, did

114

not exist at that time. The repression and defeats of 1963–64 had traumatised the party's natural supporters and who could blame them for feeling shaken? The split did not inspire confidence. If even Iraq's communists could not agree on the means to be used and the timing, it was unlikely that the Kurdish Democratic Party or others would be drawn in. Armed struggle itself was nothing new in Kurdistan, but the Kurdish leaders did not want to provoke a new bloodbath.

The armed movement launched in southern Iraq turned out to be stillborn and, as described in the last chapter, it led to the death of some very fine comrades, including Khalid Ahmed Zaki.[61] The split and the

---

61 Many were imprisoned and tortured. Others were threatened with torture. Aziz al-Hajj, the leader of the Central Command faction of the Iraqi Communist Party and a party theoretician of no mean repute, was arrested in a Baghdad suburb in 1969. Demoralised politically and unable to face prison and torture, he surrendered everything and agreed to recant in public. It is impossible to take a moral position on what a militant does under torture. And in many resistance movements this is well understood, which is why the leadership ensures that the fighters do not know too much. But Aziz al-Hajj was the best-known leader of the Central Command. He knew everything. He appeared on television interviewed by Mohammed al-Sahaf (later to acquire cult status in cyberspace as the Ba'athist Minister of Information during the Second Gulf War of 2003). Aziz al-Hajj now asked all members of the Central Command to support the Ba'ath. If Aziz al-Hajj had revealed everything during torture he would have been forgiven. During the period of the monarchy, this proud man had spent ten years rotting in the appalling desert prison Nuqrat al-Salman. In court he had defiantly defended his membership of the Iraqi Communist Party and was a hero to many students in that period.

It was his political capitulation that disgusted those he had convinced to take up arms and who had lost many friends and comrades as a result. He confirmed for the Ba'ath security organs the veracity of the detailed lists containing the names and addresses of his supporters, many of whom were tracked down and executed and whose families were regularly harassed. This was unnecessary and unforgivable. In his self-serving memoirs he recounts how Saddam Hussein visited him in prison and how he was provided with every facility to read and write and how Saddam's deputy brought him all forty-five volumes of Lenin's collected works in English and, to flatter him further, a former Prime Minister during the nationalist phase – a bitter opponent of communism – was sent to clean al-Hajj's prison room. And while his vanity was being massaged the Mukhabarat was arresting the people whose names he had given to them. A whole lifetime of struggle was wiped out in a day's work. His pilgrimage had taken him from orthodox communism to a version of Maoism/Guevarism, then the

plans for armed struggle were utilised by the Ba'ath leaders to frighten the army and probably hastened the Ba'athist coup of 1968. This time they were determined not to share power inside the army. It was too important an institution and the new leaders, General Hasan al-Bakr and his deputy, Saddam Hussein, proceeded rapidly to seal it off from all rival parties or currents. This was done not by bringing in political commissars from the party, but by a tribalisation of the army high command. Hasan al-Bakr and Saddam were both from Takrit, and the praetorian guard they created inside the army was recruited mainly on the basis of clan loyalties. Asad,

---

Ba'ath whom he served loyally in different capacities, most lately as Iraq's representative at UNESCO. Today his name appears regularly on Saudi-controlled websites as one of the more articulate defenders of the current occupation. If there were a Nobel Prize for Turncoats he might make the shortlist. His own account of his recantation, published in May 2002 in the London Arab paper *Azzaman uzZaman,* is slightly different:

That TV interview [of 3 April 1969], no doubt, marked the lowest point in my political life which had lasted a quarter of a century at that time. The genuine people who were angered and pained by that interview were justified. I understand and appreciate the reactions of the rank and file and all the party sympathisers who were shocked and shaken by that interview. I also understand the criticism and even the condemnation by genuine patriots. But I do not accept that the interview contributed to an increase in the repression. On the contrary it stopped it and contribute to ease the plight of the prisoners and from all tendencies and I would add that if it was not or my position, the guillotine would have reached to dozens of other comrades. [Translator's note: The guillotine had already done its work by then because of the lists he had supplied immediately after his arrest. Why can't he still face the truth?]

The beginning of the interview was the worst for my reputation, and a real trap to burn me politically and socially; Al-Sahaf surprised me by asking: Who were the leaders of the Central Command? It was a really surprising and embarrassing question, and instead of manoeuvring around the question, like saying well you know them all as they are all in jail, I went on to mention the names of some of those imprisoned, and the viewers who may not have been aware of the real situation, thought I was betraying my comrades. [Translator's note: Bastard.]

And then political questions were fired at me: your attitude to the Ba'ath and its power, the Kurdish question, and the Central Command's decision to wage the armed struggle (that is, the activities of our armed organisation). Here my answers were worse than the worst ... [Translated by F. Wahhab who did so on condition that his comments were preserved.]

Aziz Muhammad, first Secretary of the Iraqi Communist Party, and President Ahmad Hasan al-Bakr sign the fatal Ba'ath–Communist Pact in the 1970s. The result was a total political disaster for the ICP.

in Syria, used exactly the same methods to prepare his ascent to power via a coup that came two years later.[62] The dream of a strong and unified Arab nation that had inspired the formation of the Ba'ath now seemed like a bad joke. The old rhetoric was still used, but usually on official occasions. In reality everything had been reduced to the level of sordid clan and family politics. Patronage was thus institutionalised and became the tried and tested method of retaining power.

Once the new system was in place a decision had to be taken regarding the Iraqi Communist Party. Its militant wing had committed suicide. But the pro-Moscow faction was still in place and particularly strong in Kurdistan. Saddam Hussein and Hasan al-Bakr decided that the best way to deal with the problem was by bringing the communists out into the open. Then they could be either bought off and integrated or, when it became necessary, rounded up and destroyed. This degree of cynicism may not have infected the entire membership of the Ba'ath, but there is

---

62 Soon after Asad was appointed Minister of Defence, the Alawite sect to which he belonged began to supply the High Command of the entire armed forces in Syria as well as senior positions inside the dreaded Mukhabarat. For chapter and verse see Batatu, *Syria's Peasantry*, op cit.

little doubt that this was the plan hatched by the man who had been in charge of the security wing of the party for over a decade, and Saddam won the rest of the leadership to this view without any difficulty. The communist leaders debated at length whether to accept the offer made to them and join a national front with the Ba'ath. They were being asked to sup with the devil, but not allowed to bring a spoon. They prevaricated. They insisted on their own conditions. They screamed with rage. But since they did not reject the offer outright they were trapped like mice and the Saddam cat was watching their every movement.

In the meantime the Ba'ath regime developed close relations with the Soviet Union, trade agreements with Poland, and recognised the German Democratic Republic, which in those days was regarded as the acid test for determining the orientation of third-world regimes. It did all this for its own reasons, but one result was a pincer movement, which trapped the local communists. Because their own politics were over-determined by the Soviet Union, they now found it difficult to criticise a murderous regime. The curtain was about to rise on the last act in the tragedy of Iraqi communism. In late 1972 they decided to accept the Ba'ath offer. The shotgun marriage was consummated in public on 17 July 1973 and greeted in the Soviet and satellite press as a tremendous leap forward. Throughout their period in office, the communists exercised no real power. They became shadow puppets. All the key decisions were taken by Hasan al-Bakr and Saddam Hussein. Nor did membership of the Progressive National Front and the government end the repression. Communist soldiers in the army were executed, party members active in factories were imprisoned for short spells to cure them of trades unionism, and while the party's daily paper continued to be published it was forced to censor itself severely. Delicate issues such as repression and Kurdistan were usually avoided. Saddam personally warned the communist leaders that no activity in the army by any party other than his own would be tolerated. The key institution in the country had become a no-go area. The experience was a disaster foretold. In their hearts, the Iraqi communists must have known it would end badly.[63]

While they were part of the regime there was a new eruption in Kurdistan. The Kurdish Democratic Party had negotiated a secret deal with the Shah of Iran, backed by the United States. In return for betraying the Iranian Kurds, the KDP leader Mustafa Barzani was showered with money and new weapons and encouraged to destabilise the Ba'ath–Communist government in Baghdad. This he proceeded to do quite effectively and, helped by Iranian irregulars, inflicted serious casualties on the Iraqi army. A desperate regime in Baghdad sent Saddam to Algiers where he met the Iranians and made territorial concessions. A public announcement was made to the effect that both countries had resolved all their differences. Had Saddam smoothed over their disagreements with a pledge to get rid of the communists from the government as soon as the Kurdish threat had been contained? This accord with the Shah undoubtedly signalled that the Iraqi Ba'ath had turned in the direction of the West and it is possible that such a promise was included.

Iran was ruthless in keeping its side of the bargain. Within fourteen days of the Algiers agreement, the Shah had sealed off the Iran–Iraq border and withdrawn all support from the Kurds. Within three weeks the rebellion had ended, and the amnesty offered by Baghdad was accepted by thousands of Kurdish guerrillas. Barzani and his family fled to Iran and the KDP suffered a serious split. Jalal Talabani denounced the tribal apoliticism of

---

63 Saadi Youssef's poem 'Exhaustion' was written much later and in another country, but it sums up the tragedy that befell the largest communist party in the Arab world:

We started off
Like two stallions galloping across the earth
And collapsed
Like the sun's shadow
In the corner of a room.

the Barzani family and formed the Popular Union of Kurdistan, pledging a return to genuine nationalism and 'socialist values', that is, acceptance of rule from Baghdad.

This was a big opportunity for Baghdad to settle for a genuine regional autonomy in Kurdistan. Instead they appointed a parliament from above and began the forced resettlement of Kurds living near the Turkish and Iranian frontiers to destinations in the southern regions of the country. Reminiscent of Stalin's deportations of the Crimean Tatars and the Volga Germans from their traditional homelands or the massive expulsion of ethnic Germans from Eastern Europe after the Second World War, these arbitrary and capricious expulsions of Kurds and the levelling of their villages created resentments that are still alive.[64] The Iraqi Communist Party protested and its press began to mildly denounce these and other measures.

Saddam began to prepare a personal take-over of the country. In order to do this he had to dump the Iraqi communists and root out everyone inside the Ba'ath who might challenge his ascent. Both operations were mounted in 1978. The Ba'athists were purged in an unusual way. Saddam

---

64   The collapse of the Ottoman Empire and the creation of new states by its successors had left the Kurds stranded. After the First World War, they were the one nation desperate for their own state and an entity uniting the Kurdish people of Turkey, Iraq, and Iran was certainly possible, but it was not in the interests of the British Empire at that time. They were busy elsewhere and the Kurdish nation had nothing to offer. Since that time the Kurds of Iraq and Iran have been used, abused and disabused with a stunning regularity. The Turkish republic at least has the merit of consistency. They were integrists from the beginning. Their model was that of the French republic. Citizenship, yes, nations, no. The Kurds were denied the use of their language and brutally repressed. Since Turkey was a member of NATO and any other security arrangements deemed necessary by the US (the Baghdad Pact and after its collapse CENTO), they paid no attention to the condition of the Turkish Kurds while using the Iraqi Kurds when it suited their purposes. The result was to make the Turkish PKK extremely hard-line, but also extremely principled in not permitting itself to be used by foreign powers. The Iraqi Kurds were never denied the use of their language or education, but their dominant organisation remained stubbornly tribal in its functioning and attitudes and happy to sell itself to the highest bidder: Iran, Israel, and yes, even Baghdad.

and Asad decided on a temporary *rapprochement* and began to discuss uniting both parties and states. Neither was serious and the engagement was soon broken off by mutual agreement. But Saddam had made a note of all the Ba'athists who became over-eager for the union. Some had even been overheard saying that they preferred Asad as the leader of the new unified state rather than the Takriti. These potential dissidents were removed from the party and, in some cases, despatched altogether. That same year the Iraqi Communist Party was expelled from the government, which it never should have joined, and the National Progressive Front and some of its leaders were imprisoned. And to demonstrate the finality of this break to their new friends in Washington, Saddam Hussein had thirty-one members of the Communist Party executed on the pretext that they had ignored repeated warnings and set up party cells in the armed forces.[65] This was not the case. The post-1973 party was a broken reed, its leaders completely subservient to Moscow and by extension to the Ba'ath regime. Having joined the government they compounded the error by staying inside despite the repression of their own members and waiting patiently for the Ba'athists to eject them. This was a different party from the one that had been created and led by Fahd and Husain ar-Radi. They were men of implacable temperament and had the genuine respect of rank-and-file members. The leaders who took the party into a government over which they had no control had become demoralised creatures of the apparatus. When the Ba'ath finally dumped them there was little public sympathy for the abandoned communists. Partially this was due to the institutionalised de-politicisation of the population, which was already well under way, and partially it was due to the prevalent feeling that the Communist Party itself had become de-politicised.

---

65 Not a single newspaper in the United States condemned these executions or provided detailed coverage of the repression of the Kurds.

The following year, 1979, Saddam appointed himself a general and soon after was anointed as President of the Republic after the induced retirement of his kinsman, Hasan al-Bakr. This was not a popular decision even inside the truncated leadership of the Iraqi Ba'ath, but events conspired in Saddam's favour. That same year the Shah of Iran had been toppled by a popular revolution dominated by Shia clerics, and the United States was desperately in search of a regional replacement. Might Saddam suffice? He might. He was certainly brutal enough. He had shown this by his robust treatment of Kurds, communists, and clerics. Could he be trusted? Perhaps not, but then who could be trusted in that world any more, apart from the Saudi monarchy, whose loyalty was beyond reproach?

For his part Saddam Hussein was driven by contradictory desires. On the one hand he was prepared to play games with Washington; each side believed it was using the other in order to advance its own interests. Simultaneously, Saddam Hussein craved legitimacy in the Arab world at large. His Ba'ath rivals in Damascus had fought in the 1967 War and were active in the Lebanon. Iraq, under Ba'ath leadership, had pledged support to the PLO in Jordan, but had watched passively in 1970 as the Jordanian army crushed and destroyed the Palestinians.[66] Nuri al-Said had done the same in 1948 when the Palestinians were being driven out of their homeland. This blotted

---

66 Worried that the Jordanians might not succeed on their own and that a direct Israeli intervention might topple the monarchy, the Defense Intelligence Agency (DIA) of the United States had helpfully organised a contingent of Pakistani soldiers and officers to help out. They would, of course, be paid and at triple the rate of pay they received in Pakistan. Brigadier Zia-ul-Haq, who commanded this mercenary detachment, played a 'heroic' role in the events of Black September 1970 and was awarded the highest Jordanian honour, a kiss on the cheeks from a grateful king. His real reward came when the DIA propelled him to power in Pakistan in 1977. By that time he was already a general and Chief of Staff and he proceeded to brutalise the political culture of the country. He was also, in the imperial argot of today, the 'father of terrorism' since all the groups currently plaguing Washington (including a large chunk of the al-Qaeda High Command) were created on his watch and with his direct approval. In 1989 he was blown up in a military plane together with the US Ambassador and the latter's dog. The dog, a familiar fixture on Islamabad's diplomatic circuit, was genuinely missed.

record was not forgotten. Asad regularly taunted the Iraqi leaders for their 'courage' and the Palestinians were openly contemptuous.

Saddam was both creature and master of the Ba'athist apparatus. He had risen to power by displaying certain specialist organisational skills inside the party. He was a skilful manipulator, self-taught in the art of dividing his enemies and weakening them till they fell apart. He had done this to the communists and rival Ba'athists, attempted it (not without some success) with the Kurds and Shia clerics. He was now confident that these skills could be deployed globally. He would play with both Big Powers and use their rivalry to good effect. Saddam Hussein was neither an intellectual like Aflaq nor a mass leader like Fuad al-Rikabi. And yet he was desperate for the adulation of the people. Nor was he an original in any sense of the word. Even the personality cult he instituted was modelled on that of Stalin, Mao, and Kim il-Sung. But the person he really yearned to be was Gamal Abdel Nasser. The Egyptian leader was long dead, but his memory was still revered on the Arab street. Saddam Hussein wanted to fill the vacuum. The change of regime in Iran offered an opportunity to fulfil all his ambitions. War with Iran would please the United States, ease the fears of Saudi Arabia and the Gulf states (on the verge of a nervous breakdown lest the Iranian infection spread), and show Syria who was master. There were also domestic calculations. Having crushed virtually every single opposition, barring the Kurds, the Iraqi leader sought legitimacy. He thought a quick victory against Iran would make his position impregnable and would unite Iraqis behind the regime.[67]

---

67 The fact that domestic considerations usually influence foreign policy is often underestimated. But it applies to great empires as much as to weaker entities. Commenting on the usefulness of the First World War as a patriotic diversion from unpatriotic strikes and anti-imperialist struggles, *The Economist* of 31 March 1917 noted: 'Just as in July, 1914, in the political sphere, the country was drifting into civil war over the Irish controversy, so in the industrial sphere we were approaching general strikes upon a scale which could scarcely have been distinguished from civil war. … We were upon the edge of serious industrial disturbance when the war saved us by teaching employers and men the obligation of a common patriotism.'

There were other more serious reasons. Khomeini had begun to denounce the Iraqi government as a 'satanic regime' that repressed the Believers (the Shia constitute a large majority of Iraq's population) and called on the people to take power.[68] According to him, there could be no stability in the region unless the Iraqi Ba'athists were overthrown. In fact, the rhetoric deployed by the Ayatollah in Teheran in 1979–80 was not too different in content from the Bush–Rumsfeld–Powell–Blair propaganda prior to the war and occupation of Iraq in 2003.

The fervour of the Islamic revolution had undoubtedly excited the Iraqi mullahs in Najaf and Kerbala. There was an attempt by Shia militants to assassinate Tariq Aziz and some lesser-known leaders. The Ba'athists responded with fury and clamped down on all religious groups in the south. For the first time in Iraqi history, senior clerics were executed. Thousands of pro-Teheran activists and, no doubt, many who were not, were rounded up and deported to Iran. The regime alleged they were 'Iranian Shia' who had infiltrated Iraq, something that everyone knew was a total fiction.

In reality there was no automatic sympathy for the Iranian regime on the part of the Iraqi Shia. The identity of the latter had never been determined exclusively by their religious affinities. Other factors – clan, class, history – had been equally and often more important. The early leaders of the Ba'ath had themselves once been predominantly of Shia origin. A majority of the Central Committee of the Iraqi Communist Party was composed of Shia and the party had inherited a strong tradition of rebellion in Nasiriyah, Basrah, and the southern marshes. The collapse of other

---

68 Khomeini, who had been given refuge in Najaf after the Shah expelled him from Iran, was well aware that he was being asked to leave Iraq in 1977 because of the Washington-approved Iraq–Iran pact agreed in Algiers in 1975. What might have happened if he had been allowed to remain in Najaf remains a tantalising question.

alternatives did push many (not just the Shia) in the direction of religion, but despite this most Iraqi Shia regarded themselves first as citizens of Iraq. They did so despite the regime. If the Shia soldiers in the Iraqi army had not remained loyal, the Iranians would have crushed Iraq militarily in the war that was about to take place.

On 17 September 1980 Iraq unilaterally abrogated the Iran–Iraq frontier agreement of 1975 that had been agreed in Algiers. On the pretext that he was now determined to reassert Iraq's territorial claims, Saddam Hussein ordered the Iraqi army to cross the border with Iran in order to seize Iranian territory. Simultaneously the Iraqi air force carried out strikes on Iranian airfields. The Iraqi leadership had assumed, on the basis of intelligence supplied by Iranian royalist generals, that Iran was in a state of post-revolutionary chaos and that the entire command structure of its armed forces had been severely damaged: thousands of senior and middle-ranking officers were in prison. The assumption was that resistance would be confined to inexperienced militias, the Iraqi army would sweep through the country and it would get rid of the mullahs. This was a very serious miscalculation.

In Iran the President, Bani Sadr, realised immediately that neither religious demagogy nor the fanaticism of the revolutionary guards would be able to save the revolution. He convinced Khomeini to reconstruct the shattered army and air force and rebuild the morale of the men and their commanders. Several hundred officers were released from prison and began to reorganise the command structure of the armed forces. The global configuration of forces in relation to this conflict was a bit surreal. The Iraqi military and air force had been equipped largely by the Soviet Union,[69] while their Iranian counterparts had the latest and most sophisticated

---

[69] The Soviet Union or USSR (Union of Soviet Socialist Republics) came into existence after the 1917 Bolshevik Revolution in Tsarist Russia. After the Second World War (1939–45)

weaponry, which their royal predecessor had bought from the United States. The local satrapies were backing Iraq, and a scion of the Kuwaiti ruling family had even penned a poem referring to Saddam as the 'sword of the Arabs'. Behind the scenes, but visible, the United States and Britain were supporting Iraq. Washington, in particular, did not want the Iraqi regime to crumble and at a later stage intervened in the war by destroying an Iranian airliner carrying civilians, an error for which no apology was ever made. On the other side both Ghaddafi of Libya and Asad of Syria gave open support to Khomeini, while the Israelis did so quietly, making sure that spare parts for Chieftain tanks and damaged jets reached Teheran as quickly and quietly as possible.[70] The Israelis, ever since 1973, had viewed the Iraqi army as the most serious remaining threat in the region.

It was Iranian fighter aircraft that were decisive in the early period of the war once Iraqi raids had failed to destroy them on the ground. By late June 1982 it had become clear in Baghdad that the 'short, sharp war' they had

---

it appeared to be a permanent feature of the global landscape, with Eastern Europe under its control and successful relations in China, Vietnam, Korea, and Cuba. The period 1917–1989 was marked by wars both hot and cold and a permanent economic confrontation between the two power blocs in which each sought to strengthen its bases in countries aligned to neither. The collapse of this order began with the Sino-Soviet split in 1965 and ended in 1990 when the bulk of the middle cadres of the Communist Party of the Soviet Union decided to break with the past and became converts to capitalism without changing too many old habits. The break-up of the old Soviet Union led to the emergence of new states, most of which now have a US military presence. A former secret policeman is currently the elected President of Russia, while the son of a former secret policeman is the partially elected President of the United States. Interestingly, the implosion of the Soviet system has led to a serious weakening of democratic institutions and a strengthening of the big corporations throughout North America and the Eurozone. An inability to supply sizeable sections of their own respective populations with everyday basic needs such as effective health and education systems makes it unlikely that the United States or Britain will be able to transform Iraq (leave alone Afghanistan) into a New Deal paradise.

70   In public the old rogue Menachim Begin would say, 'When *goyim* fight *goyim*, we sit and we watch,' but this was only for domestic consumption. It suited both the Israelis and the Iranian mullahs to keep their deals a secret.

been promised was becoming more and more protracted. The leadership of the Ba'ath met and overruled Saddam Hussein. Against all his entreaties and threats it was agreed to offer a unilateral cease-fire to the Iranians. This would entail a return to the pre-war borders and the 1975 agreement. If the Iranians had accepted this offer, few doubt that Saddam Hussein would have fallen from power. But Khomeini was now in an obdurate mood. The old man was unwell and, therefore, in a hurry. He wanted to defeat the Iraqi Ba'ath and institute a regime on the Iranian model. Teheran rejected the cease-fire. In 1984, Saddam Hussein himself pleaded for a cease-fire and suggested meeting Khomeini in a neutral location. The Ayatollah once again turned down the offer and issued the following stern warning to Iraq's regional supporters: 'All of you are partners in the adventurism and crimes created by the United States. We have not yet engaged in any action that would engulf the entire region in blood and fire, making it totally unstable. You can be sure you will be the losers in this new chapter.'[71]

The propaganda used by each side accused the other of racism and unbelief. The Iraqi press highlighted the links with Israel, often publishing cartoons of Khomeini and Begin and accusing the Iranians of being 'subservient to Zionism' and 'spiteful charlatans'. Teheran responded in kind referring to the 'Ba'ath–Zionist gang' and more than once referring to the Ba'athists as the 'cursed aflaqis who have waged this war …'.[72]

---

71 Efraim Karsh, *The Iran-Iraq War: Impact and Implications*, London, 1989, p. 130.

72 This was a crude, if effective, pun on the name of Michel Aflaq, the founder of the Ba'ath Party. 'Aflaq' in Arabic also means female genitals or c*nt. Ba'ath supporters were not unused to this from local rivals in Iraq or Syria. If they replied that Aflaq was not an Arab name it affected their nationalist credentials; if they accepted it was an Arab name, their opponents would smile and say, 'It should be the name of your party.' For Iranian radio to hurl this abuse was brave, given that Syria was backing them, though Asad's hostility to Aflaq was well known.

The death toll continued to rise. As the war continued, the arms merchants of the West competed with each other to sell and supply the latest weaponry. In the first year of the war, the French had offered Baghdad a test run of their Super Étendard aircraft armed with Exocet missiles. These had worked well and the Iraqis now decided to buy thirty Mirage F-1 fighter jets and a large stock of Exocets (in addition to replenishing their old armoury with new stock from the Soviet Union). These were now used to unleash a new barrage against shipping.

The conflict continued for six more years. It was reminiscent of the First World War. Territory shifted hands regularly as tank units from opposing armies rolled over fields full of corpses. For both sides the lives of ordinary soldiers, including teenage children, were considered expendable. Dead bodies were swept aside like autumn leaves. Poison gas was used by Iraq against the Iranians and the Kurds (who the regime alleged were fighting alongside Teheran).[73] The loss of life was horrendous. And yet the war was allowed to continue as if it suited everyone to watch these two Muslim states weakening each other with every passing month. The indifference of the Islamic states was on a par with the paralysis afflicting the United Nations.

When the eight-year war finally came to an end in August 1988, only the arms merchants were unhappy. The social infrastructure of both countries was wrecked and neither properly recovered. The following casualty figures are only estimates and it is probable that many more died,

---

73 Was there a big outcry in the US or British press against chemical weapons? Was the Security Council convened to send in inspectors? Were sanctions threatened? Perish the thought. The weapons and the training were both supplied by the West. Did the Left, which opposed the 2003 war/occupation protest at that time? It did. I remember picketing the Iraqi Embassy in the company of Jeremy Corbyn, numerous Kurds, and others. It was only when Saddam Hussein was deemed an enemy of Western interests in the region after 1990 that his use of chemical weapons was ever raised seriously in the Western media by the guardians of probity.

but these approximations are bad enough. 262,000 Iranians and 105,000 Iraqis perished in the conflict. At least 700,000 were injured, which meant a combined total of over a million casualties. The financial costs were also appalling: Iraq wasted US$74-US$91 billion on waging the war and UK£41.94 billion on military imports, while Iran's defence costs amounted to US$94-US$112 billion and a further expenditure of UK£11.26 billion on buying more weapons. The profit margins of the arms industry supplying these weapons during this eight-year period are not available. To this must be added the loss of income from oil and agricultural produce: the shocking sums in this case were US$561 billion and US$627 billion for Iraq and Iran respectively.[74] As if this was not enough, both sides claimed victory and both countries commemorated this war – which should never have happened and at worst should have been ended in 1982 – by distorting their worlds with the construction of ghoulish and grisly monuments: the fountain of blood in Teheran, the soldier statuaries of Basrah and the Victory Monument of the two giant crossed swords held by two giant arms in the centre of Baghdad. The swords and the arms that hold them (modelled on the arms of the Ba'ath leader himself) were cast in a British foundry in Reading.

A year after the war the ailing Khomeini was dead and the scenes of hysterical grief that marked his funeral were, in reality, the swansong of the Islamic Republic. The structures remained in place but the population was alarmed and grew increasingly alienated from the clerics. Iran did not fight another war. In Iraq, despite the disaster into which he had led his country, the Ba'ath leader survived. His personality cult grew more atrocious by the day, a substitute for real popularity. He began to think of how he could repair his lost prestige at home. Abroad it was the Iranians

---

74   Karsh, op cit.

who were reviled for a war they had never sought, largely because the Iraqi leader continued to receive Western dignitaries and corporate executives desperate for new custom. These included the well-known businessman politician Donald Rumsfeld, but he was not alone. Western business and political links with Baghdad were very strong from 1980 to 1990.

Nobody believed that Iraq or Iran had won the war. It had ended in a bloody stalemate with both regimes intact, but weakened. The Syrian leaders, in particular, openly mocked their Iraqi counterparts for their self-deception and lies and for living in the realm of fantasy. As the country was rebuilt, which it must be admitted was done rapidly – all essential services being restored within a month – an oil dispute with Kuwait began to concentrate the minds of the Iraqi leadership. Here Saddam was not alone. The existence of Kuwait as an independent entity has bothered every Iraqi ruler since the country came into existence. In 1899, in pre-oil times, Lord Curzon made a characteristic declaration informing Britain's rivals that 'we have ... entered into engagements with the still independent Sheikh of Kuwait, a proceeding which was dictated by the increasing encroachment of Turkish authority and by the incipient intrigues of other powers'. This last was a reference to the Germans and Russians, who were exploring possibilities in the region. Could Kuwait as an Ottoman vassal enter into a treaty with another Empire? It could not, but this was soon dealt with by pressuring the weakening Ottomans to accept the Convention of 1913 recognising the Anglo-Kuwaiti treaty and agreeing not to change the status quo of Kuwait. But was the newly created State of Iraq bound by an old convention signed by a now defunct empire? Their rulers appeared to think not and insisted that Kuwait was simply an extension of Basrah province.

Prior to British penetration, societies in the Gulf were divided into three interdependent groups, which co-existed in order to preserve a social order that suited them: the Bedouin nomads traversed the deserts in search of oases and pasture, but were equally ready to abandon this way of life in return for work, wages, and a sedentary existence;[75] the agriculturalists lived in oasis towns specialising in dairy products, dates, and agricultural produce; coastal dwellers had lived from pearl diving and fishing since the earliest times. The Ottoman Empire had not interfered with this pattern of existence by imposing frontiers or insisting on the hegemony of a particular tribe. It was British colonial policy that required the division of these pre-oil societies on every level: land and tribes. Of course, once the liquid gold was discovered, colonialism flourished, and favoured tribal leaders were promoted to higher positions. Colonial 'modernity' created a tribal hierarchy to preside over an archaic social structure that suited its needs. This structural engineering excluded a majority of the population, creating a material and political base for resistance. Kuwait was an early example.

As noted earlier, King Ghazi (1933–39) made regular appeals on his private radio station to the Kuwaitis, asking them to get rid of their despotic and subservient Sheikh. These broadcasts had nothing to do with Kuwaiti oil, which was yet to be discovered; the Iraqi king simply thought that this tiny sheikhdom should, for reasons of geography, form part of Iraq. The response to his appeals had been encouraging. In 1938, a proto-nationalist youth movement had emerged, demonstrated in public and demanded greater accountability. They won a temporary victory. A Legislative Council came into existence. The first resolution agreed by the Council took London by surprise. It demanded an immediate union with Iraq. The British Empire acted quickly. In Kuwait, it intervened to protect its Sheikh. In Baghdad, it gave the signal to remove the King. Whether they meant deposition or murder remains an open question. Ghazi's death was certainly fortuitous.

---

75 Abderrahman Munif's quintet, *Cities of Salt*, remains the best fictional account of oasis societies before and after the discovery of oil.

Oil was first discovered in 1938, but only began to be marketed in 1946, when it was realised that this was the largest single reservoir of oil in the world. The bulk of the Sheikh's income was invested in the City of London and the London Stock Exchange. The Sheikh and his statelet had become a vital British asset. When, a few years after the Iraqi revolution of 1958, General Qasim looked ominously in the direction of Kuwait, he came close to provoking yet another oil war.[76] In order to prevent an invasion the Kuwaitis declared their independence. The Anglo-Kuwaiti Treaty was stated to be null and void, though Britain pledged to support the Sheikh against 'external and internal' subversion, a clear indication that gunboats and gurkhas would be despatched to quell any local uprising, and something more serious would be sent if there was the threat of a foreign invasion.

Qasim staked Iraq's claim to Kuwait at a public press conference and offered to appoint the Sheikh as Governor of the Kuwait district of the province of Basrah. In words that could apply just as well to the Iraqi collaborators of today, Qasim also pledged to improve the lives of ordinary Kuwaitis as well as those who had grown rich on the oil: 'Slaves also eat and drink and live in comfortable houses, but they are sick in spirit. The slave is he who accepts humiliation and submission to the foreigner and the imperialist.' The crisis abated but not before a great deal of British sabre-rattling and Nasser's response to the same. Qasim was not intending a direct

---

76   See 'The Kuwait Incident' by Richard Gott in *Survey of International Affairs*, edited by D.C. Watt, Oxford, 1965. It is a masterful and objective survey of the 1961 crisis by a young English historian stationed at the Royal Institute of International Affairs (sic). Together with John Gittings, another gifted young scholar at the Institute, Gott began to push in directions that were not welcome. Subsequently, to the delight of some colleagues, the awkward duo decamped to join the *Guardian* and both began to lurch leftwards at an alarming pace, giving 'international affairs' a new twist. Gott announced his engagement to the Latin American revolutionary movements, while Gittings got married to the Maoist revolution in China. Both survived and, unlike the new breed of embedded jackals, have remained pretty steadfast.

annexation, but hoping to trigger a rebellion just as Ghazi had done in the 1930s. If that had happened, Qasim would not have stood by and watched.

Three decades later, Saddam Hussein thought he would annex Kuwait to boost his economy and his standing in the Arab world. It would be a replay of Nasser and the Suez Canal. He would show everyone who was master. He felt strong and confident. Iraq was friends with the West and he had bought the most advanced weaponry on offer. He invited April Glaspie, the United States Ambassador to Iraq, for a meeting and informed her that border and oil problems with Kuwait were reaching a critical point. In particular, he pointed out, accurately, that the Kuwaitis were part of a Gulf cartel that was 'cheating' OPEC by selling oil at a lower price to maintain their profits. It was this dispute within OPEC that enraged the Iraqis, whose economy was suffering because of the fall in oil prices. Iraq demanded strict compliance with OPEC quotas and compensation for oil supposedly stolen from a field claimed by Baghdad. The signals from April Glaspie, who spoke good Arabic and did not need an interpreter, were both ambiguous and misleading. She told the Iraqis that she 'understood their concerns' and stressed that the position of the United States in the Arab world remained that inter-territorial disputes should be solved by the parties concerned. This was totally in line with US policy after the collapse of their 'twin pillar' strategy of relying exclusively on Saudi Arabia and Iran to preserve US hegemony in the region. Iran had collapsed. Perhaps Iraq could become the new second pillar. This was hardly a secret discussion and Glaspie reiterated the official view. This conversation later became the subject of much critical debate, but by that time April Glaspie had virtually disappeared and, alas, no memoirs appear to be forthcoming.[77]

---

77 The historian Peter Sluglett, whose hatred for the Ba'ath sometimes affects his objectivity, wrote of this episode: '... while she may have gone so far as to give the impression that

Saudi attempts to mediate failed when Kuwait rejected all the Iraqi demands. Was this simply recklessness or had they asked and received guarantees from elsewhere? The day after the rejection, on 2 August 1990, the Iraqi army crossed the Kuwaiti frontier and took the country. The Sabah family was deposed and Kuwaiti oil installations were occupied. The regime change carried out by Saddam Hussein was undoubtedly in violation of Article 51 of the United Nations Charter, and the United States organised a coalition under the UN flag to take back Kuwait. At the time the phrase 'national sovereignty' was much in vogue. Regime changes were impermissible where oil was involved. But legality had very little to do with the Western response. Force, not law, had always determined relations between the West and the Arab world. And force had been used or threatened to impose new laws and treaties. Essentially there was a unity of opinion amongst the Western leaders that Saddam could

---

the United States would look the other way if Iraq went about adjusting its borders by taking over Kuwait's part of the Rumayla oilfield, or quietly annexing the small islands of Bubyan and Warba (which Iraq had long been anxious to lease in order to expand its coastline on the Gulf), it was surely the height of wishful thinking on Saddam Hussein's part to imagine, as was later asserted, that he was being given an American go-ahead for a full-scale invasion, let alone annexation of Kuwait.' Marion Farouk-Sluglett and Peter Sluglett, *Iraq Since 1958: From Revolution to Dictatorship*, London, 1987. In contrast see Appendix for Christopher Hitchens' demolition of the pro-war camp.

But was it wishful thinking? He had just fought a full-scale war against Iran with US and Western backing. Compared to Iran, the sheikhdom of Kuwait was a wart. If the West had trusted him to take Iran, why should they worry about Kuwait? Glaspie's 'understanding' was misread. Had she fully understood what he meant? She was not a novice. She knew what had happened in Iran. Was she sure what was being proposed was a slight shift in the border? Did she not have any idea of the historic place of Kuwait in the thinking of Iraqi rulers of every stripe? For me it is an open question whether Saddam Hussein was wrong in his assumption that Glaspie had green-lighted the invasion. Let us look at it from a slightly different angle. What if Glaspie had been firm and asked: 'Mr President, are you planning to invade Kuwait as you did Iran?' And if he nodded as he would have done she could have said: 'I must now leave to inform the State Department and will return tomorrow to resume our discussion.' If the State Department had vetoed the project and warned that it would mean a break with the West, would Saddam still have gone ahead?

not be allowed to consolidate his position because it would make Iraq the largest oil producer and the single most important country in the region, destabilising the Gulf and threatening Israel's occupation of Palestine. And now Saddam Hussein became 'Hitler', the corrupt sheikhdom of the Sabah family became 'plucky little Kuwait', and the media began to fight the Second World War all over again. All this took place in the context of the growing disintegration of the Soviet Union.[78]

By the time the Iraqis agreed to withdraw, the US-led expeditionary force was already in place and one of the most one-sided wars of the twentieth century took place. It was, in the immortal words of a US officer, a 'turkey shoot'. In gross violation of all the conventions of war, Iraq's retreating armies were destroyed as they fled Kuwait. The image of a single burnt-out Iraqi soldier, stranded in the desert, became a symbol of the massacre. It moved the English poet Tony Harrison to compose his most popular war poem, which was published in the *Guardian*. The Third Oil War had changed the balance of power in the region, but more importantly it marked the end of a crucial chapter in twentieth-century history. The post-war settlement agreed at Yalta and Potsdam after the defeat of Hitler was now dead. This war became its ghoulish wake. Despite the 'multilateralist' cover, it was obvious from the start that the United States, as the only dominant power in the world, was in the driving seat. George Bush Sr stressed this aspect when describing how, when the crisis first erupted, 'we had started self-consciously to view our actions as setting a precedent for the approaching post-Cold War world'.[79] He also

---

78 Gorbachev and his colleagues had pinned their hopes on Bush and Thatcher helping them transform Russia into a Scandinavian-style social democracy and had become powerless on the world stage. The Russian leaders saw what was happening, tried pathetically at the last minute to stop the war and failed.

79 George Bush and Brent Scowcroft, *A World Transformed*, New York, 1999, p. 400. The book, a political memoir of the first Bush's presidency, is also worth reading as an unself-conscious

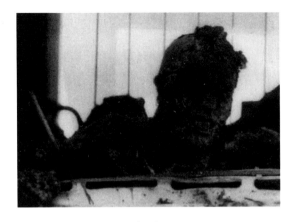

I saw the charred Iraqi lean
towards me from bomb-blasted screen,

his windscreen wiper like a pen
ready to write down thoughts for men,

his windscreen wiper like a quill
he's reaching for to make his will.

I saw the charred Iraqi lean
like someone made of Plasticine

as though he'd stopped to ask his way
and this is what I heard him say:

'Don't be afraid I've picked on you
for this exclusive interview.

Isn't it your sort of poet's task
to find words for this frightening mask?

Extracted from Tony Harrison's 'A Cold Coming'

insisted on the importance of the war because through it the US had 'kicked the Vietnam syndrome', a premature judgement. A third 'success' makes interesting reading today. At a press conference on 1 March 1991, Bush confidently asserted that the demonstration of military power would curb other acts of aggression in the future: 'I would think because of what has happened we won't have to use US forces around the world. I think when we say something is objectively correct ... people are going to listen.'[80]

One person who was certainly listening was a private Saudi citizen. Osama bin Laden had returned home from the Pamir mountains to be welcomed as a great 'freedom fighter' for his role in helping defeat the Soviet Union in Afghanistan. Some weeks after the Iraqi occupation of Kuwait, as the Saudi establishment talked of how to reverse this catastrophe, bin Laden asked for an audience with King Fahd. This was granted. During the meeting he pleaded with the King not to permit, leave alone invite, US troops to be stationed in Saudi Arabia. When Fahd inquired how he intended to eject Iraq without the Americans, Osama is reported to have informed his monarch that an armed force of 30,000 fedayeen already in Saudi Arabia was ready to go into battle and motivated enough to defeat the unbeliever Saddam Hussein.[81] The King was more shaken by this news than by the occupation of Kuwait. He hurriedly concluded

---

account of how old friendships and clan loyalties determine top appointments in the United States, confirming Hanna Batatu's remark that the Syrian Ba'athists would not be out of place in US politics.

80 Bush's son and his British junior partner appear to be infected with the same delusions. At a private, off-the-record meeting with four senior journalists from the *Guardian* after the 2003 war, Blair informed them that one major reason for the war was to make future wars unnecessary. A threat would be sufficient to bring Teheran and Pyongyang to heel. And so the war in Iraq was really a war to end all wars. A threat would be enough. This debased talk from the leader of a medium-sized Northern European country, threatening yet another country in the South, is only possible because the British Prime Minister now seems to regard the posterior of a US President as his natural habitat. And to stop this place being usurped by some other European leader justifies lies, deception, wars, etc.

81 Many of the Afghan veterans who returned home to Algeria, Egypt, Saudi Arabia, and

the interview and then turned to a minister and asked whether it was possible that Osama had an army this size already in the country. Only when he was reassured that this was all part of a fantasy did the King begin to relax again.[82] The figure, of course, may have been exaggerated, but Osama bin Laden was certainly not fibbing. His total alienation from the Saudi ruling family and the attacks of 9/11 were an unexpected minor outcome of the 1990 conflict. Blowbacks are never immediate.

Kuwait was easily 'liberated', that is, handed back to the Sabah family, and it reverted easily to its former status as a fiefdom. Saddam Hussein's adventure had made it impossible for a serious opposition to emerge in Kuwait and thousands of Palestinians were expelled. Given how the Ba'athist state functioned in Iraq it was impossible for its leaders to think creatively about Kuwait. The fact remains that the ruling family was not popular. If the Iraqis had confined their task to removing the Sabah as a ruling family, permitted free elections, and encouraged an elected assembly to determine the future of Kuwait, the operation would have been a success, making a counter-offensive by the West virtually impossible. An assembly in 1990, like the Legislative Council of 1938, might well have decided on close ties with Iraq. The Iraqi dictator could not make any effort in this direction without raising expectations in Iraq as well. Instead he went for outright annexation, which was a reckless gamble, bound to fail, given the importance of Kuwaiti oil.[83] The puzzling question is not why he

---

Pakistan were convinced that they had single-handedly defeated the Soviet Union. They ignored the central role of the Pakistani army and its US backers. This hallucinatory self-image, linked as it was to divine Providence, had imbued the Afghan veterans with an unshakeable confidence.

82   This conversation was reported to me some weeks after the events of 11 September 2001, by a senior Saudi close to his country's establishment.

83   By contrast Suharto's invasion and occupation of East Timor had been approved by the United States, but (a) they fully trusted the Indonesian dictator, (b) the Cold War was not yet over and (c) East Timor had oil reserves.

refused the Kuwaitis a free choice, but why he did not withdraw his armies once it had become obvious that the United States was planning a war to drive him out. Whatever the reasons – pride, arrogance, fantasy, stupidity – it was a callous decision. Tens of thousands of Iraqi soldiers perished.

The surrender of the Iraqi army did not lead to the fall of Saddam. The United States had no replacement ready and their Arab allies, none of whom had been elected democratically, were of the opinion that the Iraqi leader should not be removed from office. Once this was agreed, the Ba'ath leadership moved with despatch to crush the uprising in the south, which the West had initially encouraged. The Kurdish region in the north was designated a no-fly zone for the Iraqi government and regularly patrolled by US fighter aircraft.

The 'international community' now inflicted a set of punishments which were to have a devastating impact on the people of Iraq. These took the form of never-ending UN-sponsored sanctions and weekly bombing raids by Anglo-American planes. All this had the effect of making the people totally dependent on the regime for all basic necessities, strengthening the hold of the regime. As many others and I have argued in detail elsewhere, the sanctions against Iraq were a crime and the reasons given for them did not convince senior UN officials based in Iraq, who began to resign in disgust when they saw the effects of the policies they had been sent to implement.[84] It is worth repeating the statistics of a

---

84 In 1998 Dennis Halliday, the UN Humanitarian Coordinator for Iraq and a former Assistant Secretary-General, resigned in protest against sanctions, which he declared had caused deaths whose total could be upwards of a million. His successor Hans von Sponeck included civilian casualties from Clinton's and Blair's bombing raids in his brief, which enraged the bombers. Von Sponeck, too, resigned after a year because he refused to participate in punishing the people of the country and said 'that every month Iraq's social fabric shows bigger holes'. The basic reason for this was that through the Oil for Food sanctions the UN/US kept a grip on the country's throat by determining how much oil it could export. Since 1996 they had permitted the country only $4 billion of exports per year, when a

revenge directed against a whole people and justified repeatedly by George Bush, Bill Clinton, George W. Bush, and Tony Blair.

Economic sanctions reduced a population whose levels of nutrition, schooling, and public services were once well above regional standards to fathomless misery. Before 1990 the country had a per capita GNP of over $3,000. By 2001 it was under $500, making Iraq one of the poorest societies on earth. A land that once had high levels of literacy and an advanced system of health care lay ravaged by the West. Its social structure was in ruins, its people were denied the basic necessities of existence, and its soil was polluted by the use of uranium-tipped warheads, which led to a massive increase in cancers. We now know that the Defense Intelligence Agency was perfectly well aware that denying Iraq certain equipment and chemicals would lead to a water purification crisis and increase the country's death rate. This was openly discussed within the Clinton regime and approved.[85]

---

minimum of $7billion was needed to service the very reduced national provision. The 'humanitarian' supporters of sanctions could blame Saddam, but UN administrators and the Iraqi people knew that it was the West that was responsible. This helps to explain the degree of hatred encountered by the occupying armies in 2003.

85   Thomas J. Nagy, Professor at the School of Business and Public Management at George Washington University, has been single-minded in his attempts to prove that the US government deliberately targeted Iraqi civilians. His remarks below are extracted from a lengthy article in *The Progressive* magazine and an interview posted on Znet on 3 June 2003, with details of DIA websites from where the information was obtained:

Over the last two years, I've discovered documents of the Defense Intelligence Agency proving beyond a doubt that, contrary to the Geneva Convention, the US government intentionally used sanctions against Iraq to degrade the country's water supply after the Gulf War. The United States knew the cost that civilian Iraqis, mostly children, would pay, and it went ahead anyway.

The primary document, 'Iraq Water Treatment Vulnerabilities,' is dated 22 January 1991. It spells out how sanctions will prevent Iraq from supplying clean water to its citizens.

In cold language, the [Defense Intelligence Agency] document spells out what is in store: 'Iraq will suffer increasing shortages of purified water because of the lack of required chemicals and desalination membranes. Incidences of disease, including possible epidemics, will become probable unless the population were careful to boil water.' The document

What was the justification offered for this murderous reprisal against an entire people? That Saddam Hussein's regime was stockpiling weapons of mass destruction, and was about to acquire a nuclear arsenal, posing an unheard-of danger to the international community.[86] The same argument was later used to justify the 2003 war. In other words the sanctions had failed in their main aim. Even if you are the Commander-in-Chief of the USA, you can only get away with self-contradictory statements, deception and double-talk for a limited period of time, not for ever, not even with a British and Australian parrot perched on either shoulder.

Did Iraq's wars against Iran and Kuwait suggest that Saddam Hussein might unleash a pre-emptive attack against Israel, a neighbour which does possess weapons of mass destruction? This was certainly the view of the US Likudists advising the younger Bush after 9/11. It was not, however, shared by two senior realist historians of the United States. Alarmed by the war fever and the misuse of recent history, John J. Mearsheimer and Stephen M. Walt combined forces to produce a joint text for the *New York Times* in which they challenged the view being advanced by the US administration and its transatlantic allies:

---

gives a timetable for the destruction of Iraq's water supplies. 'Iraq's overall water treatment capability will suffer a slow decline, rather than a precipitous halt,' it says. 'Although Iraq is already experiencing a loss of water treatment capability, it probably will take at least six months (to June 1991) before the system is fully degraded.' This document, which was partially declassified but unpublicized in 1995, can be found on the Pentagon's website at www.gulflink.osd.mil. (I disclosed this document last fall. But the news media showed little interest in it. ... The first one in this batch is called 'Disease Information,' and is also dated 22 January 1991. At the top, it says, 'Subject: Effects of Bombing on Disease Occurrence in Baghdad.' The analysis is blunt: 'Increased incidence of diseases will be attributable to degradation of normal preventive medicine, waste disposal, water purification/distribution, electricity, and decreased ability to control disease outbreaks. Any urban area in Iraq that has received infrastructure damage will have similar problems.'
86 For further details see my text, 'Throttling Iraq', in *New Left Review* 5, September/October 2000. *The Siege of Iraq*, edited by Anthony Arnove, London, 2000, remains the most thorough analysis of the sanctions regime.

The United States faces a clear choice on Iraq: containment or preventive war. President Bush insists that containment has failed and we must prepare for war. In fact, war is not necessary. Containment has worked in the past and can work in the future, even when dealing with Saddam Hussein. The case for preventive war rests on the claim that Mr. Hussein is a reckless expansionist bent on dominating the Middle East. Indeed, he is often compared to Adolf Hitler, modern history's exemplar of serial aggression. The facts, however, tell a different story. During the 30 years that Mr. Hussein has dominated Iraq, he has initiated two wars. Iraq invaded Iran in 1980, but only after Iran's revolutionary government tried to assassinate Iraqi officials, conducted repeated border raids and tried to topple Mr. Hussein by fomenting unrest within Iraq. His decision to attack was not reckless, because Iran was isolated and widely seen as militarily weak. The war proved costly, but it ended Iran's regional ambitions and kept Mr. Hussein in power.

Iraq's invasion of Kuwait in 1990 arose from a serious dispute over oil prices and war debts and occurred only after efforts to court Mr. Hussein led the first Bush administration unwittingly to signal that Washington would not oppose an attack. Containment did not fail the first time around – it was never tried. Thus, Mr. Hussein has gone to war when he was threatened and when he thought he had a window of opportunity. These considerations do not justify Iraq's actions, but they show that Mr. Hussein is hardly a reckless aggressor who cannot be contained. In fact, Iraq has never gone to war in the face of a clear deterrent threat.[87]

---

87 *New York Times*, 2 February 2003. John J. Mearsheimer is professor of political science at the University of Chicago; Stephen J. Walt is academic dean of Harvard's John F. Kennedy School of Government. Neither man is known for leftwing or pacifist sympathies. Mearsheimer was at West Point from 1965 to 1971 and a regular participant in Armed Forces Day parades in New York in 1968, 1969, and 1971 where he was regularly pelted with pig's blood, pig's urine and other liquids by anti-Vietnam war demonstrators.

This last sentence was absolutely true and needed to be stressed. In fact, the arguments being provided by Donald Rumsfeld at the Pentagon, Colin Powell at the State Department, and Tony Blair in Downing Street did not deserve to be taken at face value. They were the first shots in a propaganda offensive to justify a war that had already been agreed.[88] This was certainly the opinion of many of us who were actively engaged in the world-wide antiwar movement. For the six months leading up to the war I argued that this was a war only partially about oil, leave alone human rights, but was essentially a war to assert imperial hegemony.[89] Increasingly this was also the view of many who argued in favour of the war. Sandwiched happily between both these views were jackals of every nationality, who had suddenly discovered that imperialism was a better option for Iraq and would impose a kinder and more beneficial regime. Such a view, as I will argue in the next two chapters, brushed against the grain of both history and current realities.

---

88   Clare Short, a member of the Blair Cabinet, was uneasy about the war and threatened to resign before it took place, but was flattered into staying by being promised that she and her department were vital for reconstruction. The cynicism was breathtaking on both sides. After the war, Short did resign or was encouraged to leave (depending on which side one is on) and later informed a House of Commons Select Committee that Bush and Blair had agreed 'in secret' to make this war regardless of all else. Falsifying evidence is hardly new in the annals of war. Recent examples include the faked Gulf of Tonkin incident of 1964, used by then-President Lyndon Johnson to start bombing North Vietnam. More recently, Clinton and Blair and their foreign ministers, Cook and Albright, intervened actively to make a deal at Rambouillet impossible so that they could wage war on Yugoslavia.

89   I argued, for instance, that this war was 'not predicated on self-defence (Afghanistan) or on the protection of others (Bosnia, Kosovo). Rather it is a crude attempt to impose US hegemony on a strategically important region – and if it succeeds will establish a dangerous new precedent for the 21st century. Pre-emptive strikes were the favoured weapons of Hitler and Mussolini in the 1930s, mimicked many years later by Israel in 1967. If the United States were to occupy Iraq, the impact of such an event could de-stabilise the entire post-cold-war-order …' *Newsweek*, 10 March 2003, p. 28.

6

WAR AND EMPIRE

On 15 February 2003, over eight million people marched on the streets of five continents against a war that had not yet begun. This first truly global mobilization – unprecedented in size, scope, and scale – sought to head off the occupation of Iraq being plotted in the Pentagon. The turnout in Western Europe broke all records: three million in Rome, two million in Spain, a million and a half in London, half a million in Berlin, over a hundred thousand in Paris, Brussels, and Athens. In Istanbul, where the local authorities vetoed a protest march in the name of 'national security', the peace movement called a press conference to denounce the ban – to which ten thousand 'journalists' turned up. In the United States there were mass demonstrations in New York, San Francisco, Chicago, and LA, and smaller assemblies in virtually every state capital: over a million people in all. Another half a million marched in Canada. The Antipodean wing of the movement assembled half a million in Sydney and a quarter of a million in Melbourne. In Calcutta, three hundred thousand people came out on the streets.

On 21 March, as British and American forces headed across the Iraqi border, the long-quiescent Arab street, inspired by these global protests, came to life with spontaneous mass demonstrations in Cairo, Sanaa, and Amman. In Egypt, the mercenary regime of Hosni Mubarak panicked and arrested over eight hundred people, some of whom were viciously maltreated in prison. In the Yemen, over thirty thousand people marched against the war; a sizeable contingent made for the US Embassy and had to be stopped with bullets. Two people were killed and scores injured. In the Israeli–American protectorate of Jordan, the monarchy had already crushed a virtual uprising in a border town and now proceeded to brutalise demonstrators in the capital. In the Arab world the tone of the streets was defiantly nationalist – 'Where is *our* army?' cried Cairene protesters. In Pakistan the religious parties took full advantage of the pro-US stance of the semi-secular Muslim League and the Pakistan People's Party to dominate antiwar mobilisations in Peshawar and Karachi. Islamists in Kenya and Nigeria did the same, though with more effect: the US embassies in both countries had to be evacuated. In Indonesia, over two hundred thousand people of every political hue marched through the streets of Jakarta.

Less than a century ago, over eight million votes were cast for the European Social Democratic parties of the Second International, inspiring the only previous attempt at co-ordinated action to prevent a war. In November 1912 an emergency conference of the International was convened beneath the Gothic arches of the old Cathedral in Basle, in an effort to avert the looming catastrophe of the First World War. As the delegates entered they were treated to a rendering of Bach's Mass in B Minor, which marked the high point of the gathering. The socialist leaders – German, British, and French – pledged to resist each and every aggressive policy of their respective governments. It was agreed that, when the time came, their parliamentary deputies would vote against war credits. Keir Hardie's call for an 'international revolutionary strike against the war' was applauded, though not put to the vote. Jean Jaurès was loudly cheered when he pointed out 'how much smaller a sacrifice a revolution would involve, when compared to the war they are preparing'. Victor Adler then read the resolution, which was unanimously approved. It concluded: 'Let the capitalist world of exploitation and mass murder be confronted by the proletarian world of peace and international brotherhood.'

By August 1914 these worthy sentiments had crumbled before the trumpet blast of nationalism. The programmatic clarity displayed at Basle evaporated as the tocsin rallied the citizens of each state for war. No credits were refused; no strike was called or revolution fomented. Amid a growing storm of chauvinist hysteria, Jaurès was assassinated by a pro-war fanatic. While a brave, bedraggled minority gathered unnoticed in the Swiss town of Zimmerwald to call for the imperialist war to be turned 'into a civil war, against reaction at home', the majority of Social Democratic leaders stood stiffly to attention as their supporters donned their respective colours and proceeded to slaughter each other. Over ten million perished on the battlefields of Europe to defend their respective capitalisms, in a conflict that saw a new Great Power make its entrance on the world stage. A century later, the United States of America had seen off virtually every rival to become the lead, often the solo, actor in every international drama.

The eight million and more who marched in 2003 were not mobilised by any International, nor did they share a common programmatic outlook. From many different political and social backgrounds, they were united only by the desire to prevent the imperialist invasion of an oil-rich Arab country in a region already riven by a colonial war in Palestine. Instinctively, most of those who marched did so because they rejected the official justifications for the bloodshed. It is difficult for those who accept these motives as 'plausible' to understand the depth of resistance they provoked and the hatred felt by so many young people for their propagators. Outside the United States, few believed that the fiercely secular Ba'ath Party of Iraq had any links with al-Qaeda. As for 'weapons of mass destruction', the only nuclear stockpile in the region is situated in Israel;

and, as Condoleezza Rice herself had pointed out in the final year of the Clinton administration, even if Saddam Hussein had such an arsenal, he would be unable to deploy it: 'If they do acquire WMD, their weapons will be unusable because any attempt to use them will bring national obliteration.'[90] Any WMDs he might have had were unusable in 2000; but three years later Saddam had to be removed by the despatch of a massive Anglo-American expeditionary force and the cluster-bombing of Iraq's cities before he got them. The pretext not only failed to convince but served rather to fuel a broad-based opposition as millions now saw the greatest threat to peace coming, not from the depleted armouries of decaying dictatorships, but from the rotten heart of the American Empire and its satrapies, Israel and Britain. It is awareness of these realities that has begun to radicalise a new generation.

Nonetheless the central argument of the Bush administration and its London sidekick centred on the necessity to disarm the Iraqi regime. President Bush, backed by tame television networks, had been stressing the weapons issue for seven months prior to the invasion. The propaganda descended upon the American public like a slagheap, but outside that country few believed the grotesque exaggerations. Nonetheless the White House persisted, and Bush's speechwriters were kept busy on this theme as is revealed by the following compilation:

'Right now, Iraq is expanding and improving facilities that were used for the production of biological weapons.'

United Nations address
12 September 2002

---

90   Condoleezza Rice, 'Promoting the National Interest', *Foreign Affairs*, January–February 2000.

'Iraq has stockpiled biological and chemical weapons, and is rebuilding the facilities used to make more of those weapons.'

'We have sources that tell us that Saddam Hussein recently authorized Iraqi field commanders to use chemical weapons – the very weapons the dictator tells us he does not have.'

Radio address
5 October 2002

'The Iraqi regime ... possesses and produces chemical and biological weapons. It is seeking nuclear weapons.'

'We know that the regime has produced thousands of tons of chemical agents, including mustard gas, sarin nerve gas, VX nerve gas.'

'We've also discovered through intelligence that Iraq has a growing fleet of manned and unmanned aerial vehicles that could be used to disperse chemical or biological weapons across broad areas. We're concerned that Iraq is exploring ways of using these UAVS for missions targeting the United States.'

'The evidence indicates that Iraq is reconstituting its nuclear weapons program. Saddam Hussein has held numerous meetings with Iraqi nuclear scientists, a group he calls his "nuclear mujahideen" – his nuclear holy warriors. Satellite photographs reveal that Iraq is rebuilding facilities at sites that have been part of its nuclear program in the past. Iraq has attempted to purchase high-strength aluminum tubes and other equipment needed for gas centrifuges, which are used to enrich uranium for nuclear weapons.'

Cincinnati, Ohio, speech
7 October 2002

'Our intelligence officials estimate that Saddam Hussein had the materials to produce as much as 500 tons of sarin, mustard and VX nerve agent.'

State of the Union address
28 January 2003

'Intelligence gathered by this and other governments leaves no doubt that the Iraq regime continues to possess and conceal some of the most lethal weapons ever devised.'

Address to the nation
17 March 2003

In London, the British Prime Minister dutifully parroted this line. He took on himself the task of preparing a special dossier to strengthen the claim, a dossier that would accompany him to Texas for the first of the war summits with his Commander-in-Chief. But he left without the dossier since British intelligence refused to manufacture the necessary information. Subsequently the department of propaganda headed by Alastair Campbell at 10 Downing Street hurriedly cobbled together a file containing half-truths, speculation, and straightforward lies, which researchers had found when they typed the magic words on *google.com*. The importance attached to the British effort in Washington was in itself an indication that not much evidence existed in the United States. There was not much in London either, but the British Prime Minister was regarded as a more convincing actor than Bush. On 18 March 2003, Blair repeated the mantra: 'We are asked to accept Saddam decided to destroy those weapons. I say that such a claim is palpably absurd.' But this is exactly the claim made by Donald Rumsfeld soon after the capture of Baghdad. Nevertheless, the British Prime Minister and his Foreign and Defence secretaries continued to repeat the 'weapons of mass destruction justification' ad nauseam after the fall of Baghdad, provoking an astonishing response from Sir Rodric Braithwaite, former head of the Joint Intelligence Committee and a former National Security Adviser to Blair at No 10. Downing Street. In a letter to the *Financial Times* of 10 July 2003, Braithwaite wrote as follows:

If the current row rumbles on, demands for a judicial inquiry into the government's handling of intelligence on Iraq will doubtless grow. Meanwhile, there is little point in speculating on what an inquiry might turn up or its likely effects on the prime minister's fortunes.

But the campaign to win round a sceptical public was not conducted primarily on the basis of intelligence dossiers. In the first months of this year we were bombarded with warnings that British cities might at any moment face a massive terrorist attack. Housewives were officially advised to lay in stocks of food and water. Tanks were sent to Heathrow airport. People were unwilling to go to war to uphold the authority of the United Nations, to overthrow an evil dictator in a distant country, or promote democracy throughout the Middle East. But in this atmosphere of near hysteria, they began to believe that Britain itself was under imminent threat and that we should get our blow in first. And so the prime minister managed – just – to swing parliament behind him.

What has happened since then? No weapons of mass destruction have been found. If they exist, they were so deeply hidden as to constitute no imminent threat to Britain. Official warnings of terrorist attacks on our cities have died away, though the incentives for terrorists to attack us have probably been increased, not diminished, by the outcome of the war. Democracy seems as far off as ever from the troubled streets of Baghdad. All may yet be well. At present it does not much look like it.

Fishmongers sell fish; warmongers sell war. Both may sincerely believe in their product. The prime minister surely acted in the best of faith. But it does look as though he seriously oversold his wares. The final judgement will be delivered not by the mandarins, the judges or the politicians. It will be delivered by the consumer – the British public.

Two days later the *New York Times* entered the fray demanding a proper inquiry to determine whether 'the administration engaged in a deliberate effort to mislead the nation about the Iraqi threat'. For the first time, opinion polls in the United States conducted in July 2003 showed a majority of the country believing that it had been misled. The irony here is that Bush, Cheney, and Powell went in for these absurd pretexts to get a UN umbrella in order to help Blair win the vote on the war in the British parliament. Most of the lies originated in Britain and were despatched to help Washington maintain the fiction. Nor should one forget the isolated Hans Blix, the Chief UN Arms Inspector, who was under heavy pressure from Washington to find something. He found nothing. Later he complained that he and his team had been used by the United States to justify its going to war, and he advised other states never to accept a UN team again. It would probably be a pretext for war. It was reported in the press that

Mr Blix ... rubbed salt in the wounds. London and Washington had built the case for invading Iraq on 'very, very shaky' evidence, he said. He referred to documents alleging that Iraq had imported uranium for nuclear weapons from Niger that he later revealed to have been faked. 'I think it's been one of the disturbing elements that so much of the intelligence on which the capitals built their case seemed to have been shaky,' he said, hinting that Britain and the US might have allowed the information to surface to undermine inspections.[91]

A month later, in an interview with *Vanity Fair*, Paul Wolfowitz admitted that 'for reasons that have a lot to do with the US government bureaucracy, we settled on the one issue that everyone could agree on: weapons of mass destruction'. In Singapore a few weeks afterwards he was equally blunt. When 'asked why a nuclear power such as North Korea was being treated differently from Iraq, where hardly any weapons of mass destruction had been found, the US deputy defence minister said: "Let's look at it simply. The most important difference between North Korea and Iraq is that economically, we just had no choice in Iraq. The country swims on a sea of oil."'[92] This was only partly true. If the war had just been about oil there was nothing to prevent a *rapprochement* with Saddam Hussein, who would have dealt just as happily with US companies as he did with the French and the Russians.

In order to justify the appalling sanctions regime, which wrecked Iraq, the US argued that the weapons were probably buried in vaults underneath Saddam Hussein's palaces, since the inspectors had been denied access to these buildings. The absurdity of this claim was shown up by the US itself when Centcom in Qatar ordered the palaces to be bombed. US war leaders constantly told the American public that one danger was the possibility that Iraq's 'weapons of mass destruction' might pass into the hands of 'Islamic terrorists'. Clearly they did not themselves believe this nonsense, as demonstrated by a columnist in the *Financial Times*:

> The most scandalous example of the US administration's inability to understand this danger was its failure to secure Iraq's known civilian

91 David Usborne, 'Hans Blix vs the US: "I was undermined"', *Independent*, 23 April 2003.
92 George Wright, 'Wolfowitz: Iraq war was about oil', *Guardian*, 4 June 2003.

nuclear sites, leaving nuclear materials open to looting for almost a week after Baghdad fell. That an administration supposedly obsessed with the nuclear threat from terrorist groups could have made such an error points to a warped sense of priorities.[93]

The Republican administration utilised the national trauma of 9/11 to create a fight-terror-law-and-order patriotism in the country that minimised dissent, while it pursued an audacious imperial agenda abroad, of which the occupation of Iraq promises to be only the first step. The programme it seeks to implement was first publicised in 1997 under the rubric 'Project for the New American Century'. Its signatories included Dick Cheney, Donald Rumsfeld, Paul Wolfowitz, Jeb Bush, Zalmay Khalilzad, Elliott Abrams, and Dan Quayle, as well as such intellectual adornments as Francis Fukuyama, Midge Decter, Lewis Libby, and Norman Podhoretz. The American Empire could not afford to be complacent at the end of the Cold War, they argued: 'We seem to have forgotten the essential elements of the Reagan Administration's success: a military that is strong and ready to meet both present and future challenges; a foreign policy that boldly and purposefully promotes American principles abroad; and national leadership that accepts the United States' global responsibilities.' The language of this coterie, compared with the euphemisms of the Clinton era, is commendably direct: to preserve US hegemony, force will be used wherever and whenever necessary. European hand-wringing leaves it unmoved.

---

93   Anatol Lieven, 'Dangers of an aggressive approach to Iran', *Financial Times*, 9 June 2003, p. 21. He could have added that while failing to secure nuclear or cultural/architectural sites, senior officers were deploying Marines to dig up the mosaic of George Bush Sr from the floor of the entrance to the al-Rashid Hotel. This was temporarily replaced with a portrait of Saddam Hussein so that Marines going into the hotel would walk over the deposed leader's face.

The 2001 assault on the World Trade Center and Pentagon was thus a gift from heaven for the administration. The next day, a meeting of the National Security Council discussed whether to attack Iraq or Afghanistan, selecting the latter only after considerable debate. A year later, the aims outlined in the 'Project for the New American Century' were smoothly transferred to the 'National Security Strategy of the United States of America', issued by Bush in September 2002. The expedition to Baghdad was planned as the first flexing of the new stance.[94] Twelve years of UN blockade and Anglo-American bombing had failed to destroy the Ba'ath regime or displace its leader. There could be no better demonstration of the shift to a more offensive imperial strategy than to make an example of it now. If no single reason explains the targeting of Iraq, there is little mystery about the range of calculations behind it. Economically, Iraq possesses the second largest reserves of cheap oil in the world; Baghdad's decision in 2000 to invoice its exports in euros rather than dollars risked imitation by Chávez in Venezuela and the Iranian mullahs; the privatization of the Iraqi wells under US control would help to weaken OPEC; strategically, the existence of an independent Arab regime in Baghdad had always been an irritation to the Israeli military – even when Saddam was an ally of the West, the IDF supplied spare parts to Teheran during the Iran–Iraq war; with the installation of Republican zealots close to Likud in key positions in Washington, the elimination of a traditional adversary became an attractive immediate goal for Jerusalem. Lastly, just as the use of nuclear weapons in Hiroshima and Nagasaki had once been a pointed demonstration of American might to the Soviet Union, so today a

---

94   In *The Right Man*, David Frum, Bush's former speechwriter, argues that: 'An American-led overthrow of Saddam Hussein – and a replacement of the radical Ba'athist dictatorship with a new government more closely aligned to the United States – would put America more wholly in charge of the region than any power since the Ottomans, or maybe the Romans.'

blitzkrieg rolling swiftly across Iraq would serve to show the world at large, and perhaps states in the Far East – China, North Korea, even Japan – in particular, that if the chips are down, the United States has, in the last resort, the means to enforce its will.

As I have stressed above, the official pretext for the war, that it was vital to eliminate Iraq's fearsome weapons of mass destruction, was so flimsy that it had to be jettisoned as an embarrassment when even famously subservient UN inspectors – a corps openly penetrated by the CIA – were unable to find any trace of them, and were reduced to pleading for more time. This might not prevent their 'discovery' after the event to save the 'credibility' of the British Prime Minister and his Cabinet, but few in Washington continue to attach much importance to this tattered scarecrow. The justification for invading Iraq now shifted to the pressing need to introduce democracy to the country – dressing up aggression as liberation. Few in the Middle East, friends or foes of the US administration, are deceived. The peoples of the Arab world view Operation Iraqi Freedom as a grisly charade, a cover for an old-fashioned European-style colonial occupation, constructed like its predecessors on the most rickety of foundations – innumerable falsehoods, cupidity, and imperial fantasies. The cynicism of current US claims to be bringing democracy to Iraq can be gauged from Colin Powell's remarks to a press briefing in 1992, when he was Chairman of the Joint Chiefs of Staff under Bush senior. This is what he had to say about the project that is ostensibly now under way:

> Saddam Hussein is a terrible person, he is a threat to his own people. I think his people would be better off with a different leader, but there is this sort of romantic notion that if Saddam Hussein got hit by a bus tomorrow, some Jeffersonian democrat is waiting in the wings to hold popular elections [laughter]. You're going to get – guess what – probably another Saddam Hussein. It will take a little while for them to

paint the pictures all over the walls again – [laughter] – but there should be no illusions about the nature of that country or its society. And the American people and all of the people who second-guess us now would have been outraged if we had gone on to Baghdad and we found ourselves in Baghdad with American soldiers patrolling the streets two years later still looking for Jefferson [laughter].[95]

This time Powell will be making sure that Jeffersonian democrats are flown in with the air-conditioning and the rest of the supplies. He knows that they may have to be guarded night and day by squads of hired American goons, like the puppet Karzai in Kabul. For the moment inter-departmental rivalry in Washington and a growing resistance in Iraq have prevented the installation of a puppet regime. The Anglo-American friends of the would-be puppet Ahmed Chalabi, all of whom loyally supported the war and occupation, were angry that their leader was effec-tively sidelined. Ahmed Chalabi arrived in Baghdad dressed in US army fatigues and was surprised at not being mobbed by a grateful populace. Given the mood in the city, he should be relieved he wasn't lynched. His supporters, also living a fantasy, toured the country tearing down Saddam's portraits and pasting Chalabi's in their place. They were surprised when most of these, too, were torn down. Today, the would-be-Nuri al-Said is one jackal amongst many. Chalabi's co-thinker, Kanaan Makiya, did not accompany the Iraqi Jefferson to Baghdad. He was being honoured in Tel Aviv, where the university gave him an honorary degree (for unsolicited favours to the State of Israel?), and he returned to the United States. From this secure haven he wrote a eulogy in the Saudi-owned Arab daily *al-Hayat* (Life), honouring the first if short-lived Viceroy of 'liberated Iraq', General

---

95   Quoted by Robert Blecher, '"Free People Will Set the Course of History": Intellectuals, Democracy and American Empire', Middle East Report Online, March 2003; *www.merip.org*.

Jim Garner. A week later, the great man had been replaced by Paul Bremer.

On the one side, a vast popular outcry against the invasion of Iraq. On the other, a US administration coolly and openly resolved on it from the start. Between them, the governments of the rest of the world. How have they reacted? London, as could be expected, acted as a bloodshot adjutant to Washington throughout. Labour imperialism was a long tradition, and Blair had already shown in the Balkan War that he could behave more like a petty mastiff, snarling at the leash, than a mere poodle. Since Britain has been bombing Iraq continuously, wing-tip to wing-tip with America under both Clinton and Bush, for as long as New Labour has been in office, only the naïve could be surprised at the dispatch of a third of the British army to the country's largest former colony in the Middle East; or the signature paltering of House of Commons 'rebels' of the stamp of Robin Cook or Clare Short or Mo Mowlem (former members of the Cabinet), regretting the violence but wishing God speed to its perpetrators.

Berlusconi in Italy and Aznar in Spain – the two most rightwing governments in Europe – were fitting partners for Blair in rallying such lesser EU fry as Portugal and Denmark to the cause, while Simitis offered Greek facilities for US spy planes. The East European states, giving a new meaning to the term 'satellite', which they had previously so long enjoyed, fell as one into line behind Bush. The ex-communist parties in power in Poland, Hungary and Albania distinguished themselves in zeal to show their new fealty – Warsaw sending a contingent to fight in Iraq, Budapest providing the training camps for Iraqi exiles, even little Tirana volunteering gallant non-combatants for the battlefield.

France and Germany, on the other hand, protested for months that they were utterly opposed to a US attack on Iraq. Schroeder had owed his narrow re-election to a pledge not to support a war on Baghdad, even were it authorised by the UN. Chirac, armed with a veto in the Security Council, was even more voluble with declarations that any unauthorised assault on the Ba'ath regime would never be accepted by France. Together, Paris and Berlin coaxed Moscow into expressing its disagreement with US plans. Even Beijing emitted a few cautious sounds of demurral. The Franco-German initiatives aroused tremendous excitement and consternation among diplomatic commentators. Here, surely, was an unprecedented rift in the Atlantic Alliance. What was to become of European unity, of NATO, of the 'international community' itself if such a disastrous split persisted? Could the very concept of the West survive? Such apprehensions were quickly to be allayed. No sooner were Tomahawk missiles lighting up the nocturnal skyline in Baghdad, and the first Iraqi civilians cut down by the Marines, than Chirac rushed to explain that France would assure smooth passage of US bombers across its airspace (as it had not done, under his own premiership, when Reagan attacked Libya), and wished 'swift success' to American arms in Iraq. Germany's cadaver-green Foreign Minister Joschka Fischer announced that his government too sincerely hoped for the 'rapid collapse' of resistance to the Anglo-US attack. Putin, not to be outdone, explained to his compatriots that, 'for economic and political reasons', Russia could only desire a decisive victory of the United States in Iraq. The parties of the Second International themselves could not have behaved more honourably.

Farther afield, the scene was very similar. In Japan, Koizumi was quicker off the mark than his European counterparts in announcing full support for the Anglo-US aggression, and promising largesse from the beleaguered Japanese taxpayer to help fund the occupation. In July 2003, Japan agreed to send troops to Iraq and help police the occupation. The new President of South Korea, Roh Moo-hyun, elected with high hopes from the country's youth as an independent radical, disgraced himself instantly by offering not only approval of the US war in the Middle East, but troops to fight it, in the infamous tradition of the dictator Park Chung Hee in the Vietnam War. If this is to be the new Seoul, Pyongyang would do well to step up its military preparations against any repetition of the same adventure in the Korean peninsula. In Latin America, the PT regime in Brazil confined itself to mumbling a few mealy-mouthed reservations, while in Chile the socialist president Ricardo Lagos – spineless even by the standards of sub-equatorial social democracy – frantically cabled his ambassador to the UN, who had irresponsibly let slip the word 'condemn' in chatting with some journalists, to issue an immediate official correction: Chile did not condemn, it merely 'regretted' the Anglo-US invasion. If only the new discourse had been in place in 1973, then we could have 'regretted' the US-sponsored coup against Salvador Allende, without 'condemning' it. After all, it could have been argued, this was an 'internal matter'. The US had not invaded the country.

In the Middle East, the landscape of hypocrisy and collusion is more familiar. But, amidst the overwhelming opposition of Arab public opinion, no client regime failed to do its duty to the paymaster-general. In Egypt Mubarak gave free passage to the US navy through the Suez Canal and airspace to the US air force, while his police were clubbing and arresting hundreds of protesters. The Saudi monarchy invited cruise missiles to arc over their territory, and US command centres to operate as normal from their soil. The Gulf states have long become virtual military annexes of Washington. Jordan, which managed to stay more or less neutral in the first Gulf War, this time eagerly supplied bases for US special forces to maraud across the border. The Iranian mullahs, as oppressive at home as they are stupid abroad, collaborated with CIA operations Afghan-style. The Arab League surpassed itself as a collective expression of ignominy, announcing its opposition to the war even as a majority of members were participating in it. This is an organisation capable of calling the Kaaba black while spraying it red, white, and blue.

The reality of the 'international community' – read: American global hegemony – has never been so clearly displayed as in this dismal panorama.

Against such a background of general connivance and betrayal, the few – very few – acts of genuine resistance stand out. The only elected body that actually attempted to stop the war was the Turkish parliament. The newly elected AKP regime performed no better than its counterparts elsewhere, cravenly bargaining for larger bribes to let Turkey be used as a platform for a US land attack on northern Iraq. But mass pressures, reflexes of national pride or pangs of conscience prompted large enough numbers of its own party to revolt and block this transaction, disrupting the Pentagon's plans. The Ankara government hastened to open airspace for US missiles and paratroop drops instead, but the action of the Turkish parliament – defying its own government, not to speak of the United States – altered the course of the war; unlike the costless Euro-gestures that evaporated into thin air when fighting began. In Indonesia, Megawati pointedly drew attention to the Emperor's clothes by calling for an emergency meeting of the Security Council to condemn the Anglo-American expedition. Naturally, after months of huffing and puffing from Paris, Berlin, and elsewhere about the sanctity of UN authority, the response was complete silence. In Malaysia, Mahathir – not for the first time breaking a diplomatic taboo – bluntly demanded the resignation of Kofi Annan for his role as a dumb-waiter for American aggression. These politicians understood better than others in the Third World that the American Empire was using its huge military arsenal to teach the South a lesson in the North's power to intimidate and control it.

The war on Iraq was planned along the lines set out by its predecessors in Yugoslavia and Afghanistan. It is clear that politicians and generals in Washington and London hoped that the Kosovo–Kabul model could essentially be repeated: massive aerial bombardment bringing the opponent to its knees without the necessity of much serious combat on the ground. In each of these cases there was no real resistance, once B-52s and daisy-cutters had done their work. But on hand to secure the right result were also the indispensable 'allies' of the targeted regimes themselves. In the Balkans it was Yeltsin's emissaries who talked Milosevic into putting his head into the American noose by withdrawing his troops intact from their bunkers in Kosovo. In Afghanistan, it was Musharraf who ensured that the bulk of Taliban forces and their Pakistani 'advisers' melted away, once Operation Enduring Freedom began. In both countries, it was the external patron whom the local regimes had relied on for protection that pulled the rug from under them.

In Iraq, however, the Ba'ath dictatorship was always a tougher and more resilient structure.[96] It had received varying diplomatic and military support from abroad at different stages of its career (including, of course, from the United States, as well as Russia), but had never been dependent on them. Confident, nevertheless, that its top command must be brittle and venal, Washington persistently tried to suborn Iraqi generals to turn their coats or, failing that, simply to assassinate Saddam himself. Once all such attempts – even at the eleventh hour – proved a fiasco, the Pentagon had no option but to launch a conventional land campaign. The economic and military strength of the American Empire was always such that, short of a rebellion at home or an Arab-wide *intifada* spreading the war throughout the region, it could be confident of pushing through a military occupation of Iraq. What it could not do was predict with any certainty the political upshot of such a massive act of force.

In the event, the Iraqi army did not disintegrate at the first shot; there was little sign of widespread popular gratitude for the invasion but rather more of guerrilla resistance and – as civilian casualties from missiles, mortars, and bombing raids mounted – of increasing anger in the Arab

---

96 When Kanaan Makiya and two fellow-quislings were granted an audience ('graciously received' in Makiya-talk) in the Oval Office last January he flattered Bush by promising 'that invading American troops would be greeted with "sweets and flowers"'. The reality turned out to be slightly different. See *New York Times*, 2 March 2003.

world. Temporarily, the Crusader armies succeeded in making Saddam Hussein a nationalist hero: his portraits flourished in demonstrations in Amman and Gaza, Cairo, and Sanaa. The hospitals of Baghdad overflowed with the wounded and dying, as the city was prised apart by American tanks. 'We own it all,'[97] declared a US colonel, surveying the shattered capital in the spirit of any Panzer commander in 1940. Behind the armoured columns, the Pentagon has an occupation regime in waiting, headed by former US General Jay Garner, an arms dealer close to the Zionist lobby at home, with assorted quislings – fraudsters and mountebanks like Ahmed Chalabi and Kanaan Makiya – in its baggage train. It will not be beyond the US authorities to confect what it can dub as a representative regime, with elections, an assembly, and so on, while the 'transitional administration' will no doubt be funded by the sale of Iraqi assets. But any illusion that this will be a smooth or peaceable affair has already vanished. Heavy repression will be needed to deal not merely with thousands of Ba'ath militants and loyalists, but with Iraqi patriotic sentiments of any kind; not to speak of the requirements for protecting collaborators from nationalist retribution.

Already the lack of any spontaneous welcome from Shi'ites and the fierce resistance of armed irregulars have prompted the theory that the Iraqis are a 'sick people' who will need protracted treatment before they can be entrusted with their own fate (if ever). Such was the line taken by the permanently embedded Blairite columnist David Aaronovitch in the *Observer*. Likewise, George Mellon in the *Wall Street Journal* warns: 'Iraq Won't Easily Recover From Saddam's Terror': 'after three decades of rule

---

97   Banner in the *Los Angeles Times*, 7 April 2003. Analogies with Hitler's blitzkrieg of 1940 were drawn without compunction by cheerleaders for the war. See Max Boot in the *Financial Times*, 2 April 2003: 'The French fought hard in 1940 – at first. But eventually the speed and ferocity of the German advance led to a total collapse. The same thing will happen in Iraq.' What took place in France after 1940 might give pause to these enthusiasts.

of the Arab equivalent of Murder Inc, Iraq is a very sick society'. To develop an 'orderly society' and re-energise (privatise) the economy will take time, he insists. On the front page of the *Sunday Times*, its reporter Mark Franchetti quoted an American NCO: "'The Iraqis are a sick people and we are the chemotherapy," said Corporal Ryan Dupre. "I am starting to hate this country. Wait till I get hold of a friggin' Iraqi. No I won't get hold of one. I'll just kill him."' The report – in Murdoch's flagship paper – goes on to describe how his unit killed not one but several Iraqi civilians later that day.[98] No doubt the 'sick society' theory will acquire greater sophistication, but it is clear the pretexts are to hand for a mixture of Guantanamo and Gaza in these newly Occupied Territories.

There will, of course, be pleas from the European governments for the UN to take over the conquests of American arms, which Blair, keener than Bush on unctuous verbiage, will second for reasons of his own. Much talk has been heard of humanitarian relief, the urgency of alleviating civilian suffering and the need for the international community to 'come together again'[99]. So long as no real power is ceded to the UN, the US has everything to gain from an *ex post facto* blessing bestowed on its aggression, much as in Kosovo. The months of shadow-boxing in the Security Council – while, in the full knowledge of all parties, Washington readied the laborious logistics for attacking Iraq – cost it little. Once it had Resolution 1441 in its pocket, passed by a unanimous vote – including France, Russia, and China, not to speak of Syria – the rest was décor. Even France's Ambassador to Washington, Jean-David Levitte, had urged the US not to go forward with the second resolution: 'Weeks before it was tabled I went to the State Department and the White House to say, "Don't do it. … You don't need it."'

---

98 *Sunday Times*, 30 March 2003.
99 *Financial Times*, 26 March 2003.

It was, of course, sanctimony in London rather than bull-headedness in Washington that dragged the world through the farce of further 'authorisation', without success. But Levitte's advice spotlights the real nature of the United Nations, which, since the end of the Cold War, has been little more than a disposable instrument of US policy. The turning-point in this transformation was the dismissal of Boutros-Ghali as Secretary-General, despite a vote in his favour by every member of the Security Council save the US, for having dared to criticise the way the West concentrated on Bosnia at the expense of far greater tragedies in Africa. Once Kofi Annan – the African Waldheim, rewarded for helping the Clinton administration to deflect aid and attention from genocide in Rwanda – was installed instead, at Washington's behest, the organisation was safely in American hands.

This does not mean it can be relied on to do the will of the US on every matter, as the failure of its efforts to secure a placebo for Blair made clear. There is no need for that. All that is necessary – and now unfailingly available – is that the UN either complies with the desires of the US, or rubber-stamps them after the event. The one thing it cannot do is condemn or obstruct them. The attack on Iraq, like the attack on Yugoslavia before it, is from one point of view a brazen violation of the UN Charter. But no member state of the Security Council dreamt of calling an emergency meeting about it, let alone moved a resolution condemning the war. In another sense, it would have been hypocrisy to do so, since the aggression unfolded logically enough from the whole vindictive framework of the UN blockade of Iraq since the First Gulf War, which had already added further hundreds of thousands of dead to the credit of the Security Council since its role in Rwanda.[100] To turn from the US to appeal to the authority of the UN is like expecting the butler to sack the master. And

---

100   For this background to the war, see 'An Ocean of Terror' in my *Clash of Fundamentalisms*.

true to form, in the last week of May 2003, the UN Security Council capitulated completely, recognised the occupation of Iraq, and approved its recolonisation. The timing of the 'mea culpa' by the 'international community' was perfect. The day after, senior executives from more than one thousand companies gathered in London to bask in the sunshine of the re-established consensus under the giant umbrella of Bechtel, the American Empire's most favoured re-construction company. It was agreed that a tiny proportion of the loot could be shared.

To point out these obvious truths is not to ignore the divisions that have arisen within the 'international community' over the war in Iraq. When the Clinton administration decided to launch its attack on Yugoslavia, it could not secure authorisation from the Security Council because Russia had cold feet; so it went ahead anyway through NATO in the correct belief that Moscow would jump on board later, and the UN would ratify the war once it was over. This time NATO itself was split so could not be used as a surrogate. But it would be unwise to assume the outcome will be very different.

This is the first occasion since the end of the Cold War when a disagreement between the inner core of the EU and the United States exploded into a public rift, was seen on television and helped polarise public opinion on both sides of the Atlantic. But only a short journalistic memory could forget that a still more dramatic dispute broke out during the Cold War itself, occasioned by the same kind of adventure in the same region. In 1956 a 'unilateralist' Anglo-French expedition, in collusion with Israel, attempted to effect regime change in Egypt – to the fury of the United States, which had not been consulted beforehand and feared the adventure might open the door to communist influence in the Middle East. When the USSR threatened to use rockets to help Nasser, Eisenhower ordered Britain to pull out of Egypt on pain of severe economic punishment, and the tripartite assault had to be abandoned.

This time the roles have been largely reversed, with France and Germany expostulating at an American expedition, in which Britain – the perpetual attack-dog – has joined.

The difference, of course, is that now there is no Soviet Union to be considered in the calculus of aggression, and overwhelming power anyway rests with the US, not Europe. But the lessons of 1956 have not lost their relevance. Sharp international disputes are perfectly compatible with a basic unity of interests among the leading capitalist powers, which quickly reasserts itself. The failure of the Suez expedition prompted France to sign the Treaty of Rome establishing the EEC, conceived in part as a counterweight to the US. But the US itself supported the creation of the European Community, whose enlargement today serves its purposes, as the French elite is becoming uneasily aware – although far too late to do much about it. Ill feeling is likely to linger between Washington and Paris or Berlin after the public friction of recent months, even if, as we are repeatedly assured, all sides will strive to put it behind them. Within the EU itself, Britain's role in backing the US against Germany and France, while pretending to play the go-between, has exposed it once again as the Trojan mule in the Community. But the days when de Gaulle could genuinely thwart the US are long gone. Chirac and Blair kissed and made up soon enough.

If it is futile to look to the United Nations or Euroland, let alone Russia or China, for any serious obstacle to US designs in the Middle East, where should resistance start? First of all, naturally, in the region itself. There, it is to be hoped that the invaders of Iraq will eventually be harried out of the country by a growing national reaction to the occupation regime they will install, and that their collaborators may meet the fate of Nuri al-Said before them. Sooner or later, the ring of corrupt and brutal tyrannies around Iraq will be broken. If there is one area where the cliché that classical revolutions are a thing of the past is likely to be proved wrong, it is the Arab world. The day the Mubarak, Hashemite, Assay, Saudi, and other dynasties are swept away by popular wrath, American – and Israeli – arrogance in the region will be over.

In the imperial homeland itself, meanwhile, opposition to the ruling system should take heart from the example of America's own past. In the closing years of the nineteenth century, Mark Twain, shocked by chauvinist reactions to the Boxer Rebellion in China and the US seizure of the Philippines, sounded the alarm. Imperialism, he declared, had to be opposed. In 1899 a mammoth assembly in Chicago established the American Anti-Imperialist League. Within two years its membership had grown to over half a million and included William James, Henry James, W. E. B. Dubois, William Dean Howells, and John Dewey. Today, when the United States is the only imperial power, the need is for a global Anti-Imperialist League. But it is the US component of such a front that would be crucial. The most effective resistance of all starts at home. The history of the rise and fall of empires teaches us that it is when their own citizens finally lose faith in the virtue of infinite war and permanent occupations that the system enters into retreat.

The World Social Forum has, till now, concentrated on the power of multinational corporations and neo-liberal institutions. But these have always rested on foundations of imperial force. Quite consistently, Friedrich von Hayek, the inspirer of the Washington Consensus was a firm believer in wars to buttress the new system, advocating the bombing of Iran in 1979 and of Argentina in 1982. The World Social Forum should take up that challenge. Why should it not campaign for the shutting down of all US military bases and facilities abroad – that is, in the hundred plus countries where the US now stations troops, aircraft or supplies? What possible justification does this vast octapoid expanse have, other than the exercise of American power? The economic concerns of the Forum are in no contradiction with such an extension of its agenda. Economics, after all, is only a concentrated form of politics, and war a continuation of both by other means.

In recent months we have been surrounded with politicians and pundits, prelates and intellectuals, parading their consciences in print or on the airwaves to explain how strongly they were opposed to the war, but now that it has been launched they believe that the best way to demonstrate their love for humanity is to call for a speedy victory by the United States, so that the Iraqis might be spared unnecessary suffering. Typically, such figures had no objection to the criminal sanctions regime, and its accompanying dose of weekly Anglo-American bombing raids, that heaped miseries on the Iraqi population for the preceding twelve years. The only merit of this sickening chorus is to make clear, by contrast, what real opposition to the conquest of Iraq involves.

The immediate tasks that face an anti-imperialist movement are support for Iraqi resistance to the Anglo-American occupation, and opposition to any and every scheme to get the UN into Iraq as retrospective cover for the invasion and after-sales service for Washington and London.[101] Let the aggressors pay the costs of their own imperial ambitions. All attempts to dress up the recolonisation of Iraq as a new League of Nations Mandate, in the style of the 1920s, should be stripped away. Blair is the leading mover in this, but there is no shortage of European extras behind him. Underlying this obscene campaign, now a common denominator on Murdoch's TV channels, the BBC and CNN, is the urgent desire to reunite the West. The vast bulk of official opinion in Europe, and a substantial chunk in the US, is desperate to begin the post-war 'healing

---

101   This was the line of the bloodstained Russian President, Vladimir Putin, during his state visit to Britain in June 2003. The conqueror of Chechnya, responsible for more Chechen deaths in six months than *all* the Kurds killed by the Iraqi Ba'ath, declared that the UN should take over Iraq, presumably so that the crony capitalists of Russia can get a share of the action, but also to cover his own exposed rear.

process'. The only possible stance to adopt in anticipation of what lies ahead is summed up in the motto heard on the streets of San Francisco in the spring of 2003: 'Neither their war nor their peace'. It is a sentiment which seems to have caught on in Baghdad and Basrah, Nasiriyah and Najaf, Amarah and Falujah and …

Since 1 May 2003, when the war officially ended, and 31 July 2003, the casualty lists have grown steadily. Every week US soldiers are killed or wounded. The British army, too, despite the PR, is finding it difficult to win popular support for its presence and, as a consequence, is sustaining losses. As a result of this low-intensity guerrilla warfare, which is *not* the exclusive responsibility of the Ba'ath, the Pentagon is anxious to involve other countries to share the burden if not the profits (which still appear remote). The declining morale of US soldiers is beginning to worry the Pentagon.

At the time of writing efforts are being made to transport contingents from the Pakistan and Indian armies to shore up the occupation. After all, they reason at Foggy Bottom, this is the historic role of these armies. They have played it well in the past. They will not require extensive or costly rehearsals. Better they fight for us than fight each other. Created by the British over a hundred years ago, how well the structures have survived. The chain of command has never been broken by unruly rebellions from below, like Syria and Iraq. What a tribute to the British Empire. Indian soldiers helped crush uprisings in the 1920s. The same regiments could be sent again and once again we could put them under British control. All sides could then bask in the memories of time past.

In Islamabad and New Delhi, the secular general and the Hindu fundamentalist ponder the request. What might be its consequences? Times have changed in Pakistan since it supplied Brigadier Zia-ul-Haq to the Jordanians to help crush the Palestinian uprising in September 1970. If Pakistani soldiers are sent to police Iraq on behalf of the Empire there will be a medium-term impact inside the army: Islamist currents will grow. Musharraf's plea that the United Nations mask might better help to conceal the reality of an imperial occupation is designed to cover himself, though few in the country will be deceived by this feint. Of course there is always the money. Pakistani soldiers and officers will be better paid than they are at home; this is always an inducement and even more so in these great times of globalisation. The fact that Pakistan's soldiery will be asked to kill co-religionists has never bothered the High Command in the past: Palestinians, Bengalis, Afghans, Baluch, and Sindhis are well aware of this fact. Iraq could easily be added to the list.

Further south, New Delhi, which was desperate to be part of the Afghan war, does not want to be left out of Iraq. Despite the public pleas of India's more distinguished secular intellectuals and journalists, the Hindu fundamentalist-led coalition was determined to bloody its soldiers in battle, but pulled back in the face of opposition from its coalition partners and the opposition. Here a modest proposal might be in order. Instead of sending official detachments from the Indian army, why not inaugurate a new type of intervention, which serves both domestic and foreign needs. An army of volunteers under the ruthless but dynamic leadership of the Narender Modi Brigade could really distinguish itself in service abroad.[102] Surely the time has come to introduce the re-elected gauleiter from Gujarat to the rest of the world. As we know only too well, atrocities perpetrated by elected governments are different from those carried out by dictators, unless elected politicians from the imperial

---

102   Modi is the Hindu fundamentalist Chief Minister of Gujarat, the Indian state in which a carefully organised pogrom against the Muslims shook the rest of the country. Modi refused to accept any responsibility, leave alone apologise. In receipt of orders from above, the Gujarat police force watched poor Muslims being slaughtered without intervening. Three thousand perished and several thousand had to flee their villages. Modi was re-elected as Chief Minister. The pathetic Congress Party had also chosen a Hindu fundamentalist to oppose him. The best-researched account of the Gujarat massacres is contained in *Gujarat: The Making of a Tragedy*, edited by Siddharth Varadarajan, New Delhi, 2002.

metropolis are instructing the latter. Modi's democratic credentials are not in doubt. Nor is his ability to go in for the kill. His police force could easily be provided with helmets and trousers – blue on the outside, pure saffron inside – and despatched to quell the angry Muslim population of Iraq. It could all be done officially, without the need to invent any fictions to justify mass slaughter.

There is a slight problem, of course, which is that the Iraqis will resist and Modi's murder squads are more used to killing unarmed Muslims. But here readjustments are surely possible. Often unarmed villagers have to be killed and their villages burnt for supplying food to the resistance. The Modi Brigade could maintain morale by specialising in this sort of operation.

7

EMPIRES AND RESISTANCE

The conquest of Iraq marks a new phase in the country's history and an ominous opening for the twenty-first century. In the West it has inaugurated a wide-ranging debate on subjects that had become unmentionable in polite society: empires and imperialism, civilisations and their discontents, capitalism and its stages, Europe versus America. And perhaps, unknown to all, an American Virgil, hidden deep in Christian country, is already hard at work composing a philippic in honour of the imperial chief (*Georgics Dubya?*), which could begin with the concluding lines of the last of the *Georgics*:

> ... great Caesar fired his lightnings and conquered
> By deep Euphrates.

Little Caesar, too, has captured by deep Tigris, but in capitalist time. Capitalism has lost its originality. It is doomed to repeat its past, albeit in changed conditions. What is new is not the American Empire, but its solitary existence. It is the first time in world history that a single Empire has become hegemonic. It was already the case after 1990, but attempts were made to camouflage reality with fine phrases: 'a new world order', the 'peace dividend', and 'a nuclear-free Europe from the

Atlantic to the Urals', etc. All this provided a happy basis for Euro-American collusion. And a few years later when it was once again time to 'exterminate all the brutes', the Euro-American alliance, also known as 'the international community', remained unruffled. Disagreements did emerge before and during the Yugoslav war but were confined to private gatherings. The decision to occupy Iraq provoked more anger and bitterness between rulers and ruled, North and South than any single event since the last phase of the Vietnam War (1960–75). Could it be that the continental West European governments had only just realised that the Monroe Doctrine had now been extended to the whole world?[103]

Academic and media apologists (often the same) for current US policies stress that this is the only way to stabilise the world and bring tyranny to heel. Far better for a country to become a US protectorate than remain an indigenous dictatorship. However, evidence for the benevolence of the United States or a happy compliance with its rule is only to be found in western Europe. Nowhere else. To imagine otherwise is to ignore the history of the twentieth century. Martin Luther King Jr spoke for whole continents when he stated that 'the greatest purveyor of violence in the world is my own country'.[104] This violence started long before the Russian Revolution, carried on during its peak and after its fall throughout the last century, and has christened the present one with the occupation

---

103   The Monroe Doctrine, first elaborated during the tenure of President Monroe in 1823, was a warning to the European colonial powers not to expand any further in the western hemisphere. This was the prerogative of the United States, and the growing military muscle of the youngest imperial power was soon sufficient to deter raiding parties from the Old World. For this and much else E.J. Hobsbawm's *The Age of Empire* remains an invaluable point of reference.

104   And the US state proved his point by approving his execution. For details on this sad story see William F. Pepper, An *Act of State: The Execution of Martin Luther King*, London and New York, 2002.

of Iraq. Since historical amnesia is encouraged by official culture, to the extent where policy-makers themselves lost sight of Iraq's past when they assumed that they would be welcomed as 'liberators', it is worth listing a few of the more violent episodes involving the United States that marked the second half of the twentieth century. This tally begins with the decision to use nuclear weapons on Japanese cities, partially as a warning to the Soviet Union not to overreach itself.

- The use of nuclear weapons on the civilian populations of Hiroshima and Nagasaki. Death toll: 2,00,000. Deaths from after-effects: not computed.

- The destruction of every building in North Korea during the 1950–53 war to destroy the whole infrastructure of the region. Death toll of Koreans (North and South): 900,000.

- The 1965 massacres in Indonesia, supported by the US intelligence agencies and carried out by pro-US military leaders. Death toll: over 1 million.

- The 1960–75 war unleashed against Vietnam and fought with the regular use of chemical weapons of which the effects of Agent Orange are still visible in the country. Death toll: 50,000 US soldiers; 2 million Vietnamese.

- The Third Oil War, 1990. Death toll: between 50,000 and 100,000 Iraqi soldiers.

- The effect of sanctions against Iraq. Death toll: up to 1 million dead.

- The 2003 war against Iraq. Not concluded.

The de facto US protectorates throughout the second half of the twentieth century have in the main constituted some of the most vicious dictator-ships in the world. These were not simply 'bad Cold War habits' as apologists have tended to claim, since the Monroe Doctrine led to unceasing interventions in Central America to secure it for US corporate interests many decades prior to the victory of Lenin's Bolsheviks.

1953: CIA helps remove Iranian democrat Mohammed Mossadegh from power as punishment for nationalising the country's oil. The Shah is put back on the throne. Massive repression of all opposition, but the mosques cannot be shut. Their doors stay open and they become centres of resistance to the regime.

1958: In order to prevent a general election, which it fears might produce a nationalist government, the CIA/DIA authorise first military coup in Pakistan. A decade of military rule leads ultimately to the break-up of the country in 1971.

1964: US Ambassador Lincoln Gordon masterminds plot for military take-over in Brazil. President João Goulart goes into exile. A slogan appears on a Rio de Janeiro wall: '*No More Middlemen! Lincoln Gordon for President!*' Widespread arrests and torture of leftists and trades-union militants.

1967: CIA operatives watch as a captured prisoner is shot dead by machine- gun bullets in Bolivia. His name is Che Guevara.

1973: US authorises General Pinochet's military coup in Chile. Elected president Salvador Allende is killed defending himself. Mass arrests and killings. Between 6,000 and 10,000 members of socialist and communist parties, peasant organisations and other left groups are 'disappeared'.

1975: US authorises Indonesian invasion of East Timor to pre-empt national independence after Portuguese withdrawal. By 1989 the occupying armies will kill over 200,000 Timorese, imprison several thousand, institute a form of slave labour, and loot the country.

1975: US supports military coup in Argentina. General Videla declares that the enemy is within and the country must be purified.

1977: DIA approves new coup in Pakistan. The country's first elected leader is charged with murder and hanged. Public hangings and floggings brutalise the country's culture and the new dictator, General Zia-ul-Haq, becomes a valued client and vital to the war in Afghanistan. Here lie the origins of al-Qaeda and other fundamentalist creations that are tearing the region apart.

1979: Closer links established with new Iraqi leader Saddam Hussein, who is armed and supported during the war with Iran, in the course of which he uses chemical weapons against a Kurdish village. Close relations continue till 1990 invasion of Kuwait.

1982: US marines invade and occupy the tiny Caribbean island of Grenada, whose Head of State (the Queen of England) is irked that she was not informed. Reagan's Secretary of State George Schultz arrives on the island and announces: 'At first sight I realised that this island could be a splendid real estate project.'

1984: US begins arming Contra forces in Nicaragua behind the backs of its own Congress to unleash a civil war and overthrow the democratically elected Sandinista regime. Ronald Reagan quotes St. Luke (14.31) to ask for money to battle the Evil Empire.

1990: The Gulf War: a 'turkey-shoot' to destroy an army in total retreat; destruction of Iraq's social infrastructure; systematic attack on Iraqi people via a criminal UN sanctions regime.

1999: NATO war against Yugoslavia.

2002: US–Spanish-backed coup attempt against Hugo Chavez in Venezuela. Chavez has won seven different elections and referendums, despite the opposition of the private TV networks and a large part of the press. The coup fails because of opposition from soldiers and the poor.

2003: US–British invasion and occupation of Iraq.

What these incomplete charts of post-1944 imperial interventions reveal is the effortless rise of the United States as the leader of the capitalist world and its determination to weaken, destroy and defeat not just the communist opponent, but also those who refused to take sides in the Cold War while maintaining their own independence. This generation of nationalist leaders is epitomised by Nehru, Nasser, Nkrumah, Lumumba, Sukarno, and from a third continent by Peron, Vargas, Goulart, Allende, and, most recently, Hugo Chavez of Venezuela.[105]

The last quarter of the nineteenth and the first half of the twentieth century was the period of the empires of Europe and Japan. Dominant among these were the British, followed by the French and Dutch and later by the Japanese and the Germans.[106] It is impossible to understand the

---

105   US hostility to nationalist-communists like Ho Chi Minh and Fidel Castro hardly needs to be recalled. In April 1975 the first of these became the only leader whose people defeated the United States. The second survived all assassination attempts and direct intervention to overthrow his regime, despite a continuous economic blockade that has lasted for almost half a century.

106   Germany only came into existence as a state in 1871. The Congress of Vienna in 1815 (the assembly of victors after the defeat of Napoleon) had ducked the German question by accepting only a loosely based German Confederation of thirty-nine states. It was left to Bismarck and Prussia to complete the process of German unification. Bismarck was unmoved by misty references to the Holy Roman Empire and Charlemagne. He defeated his Austrian rivals in 1866 and the French in 1870, thus removing two obstacles to Prussian leadership of the state-in-creation. He built a strong, unifed, no-nonsense state under Prussian leadership (Einheitsstaat). The lack of mass republicanism in the German lands made it easier for him to anoint the Prussian king as the Kaiser of the new state, a symbol of its military strength and future glory, resting on the Junkers and what became the most efficient state bureaucracy in

logic that underlay the First and Second World Wars without a grasp of imperialist history and the inter-imperialist contradictions that marked the period. Despite the rhetoric, neither of these two wars were a defence of 'democracy' against 'tyranny'. It is difficult to even claim that for the first conflict. There was a restricted franchise in most of the countries that were at war and none at all in the Ottoman and tsarist Empires. It was an inter-imperialist war provoked by greed to determine which European great power would dominate the world and be the greatest colonial power. It was generally agreed by all that Europe needed more 'living space'. The only question was who got what and on which continent.

For many decades prior to the war, the 'colonial question' had been hotly debated inside the socialist parties of Europe. The initial position was unambiguous. The 1896 Congress of the Second International had adopted a resolution proposed by George Lansbury from the British Independent Labour Party, which demanded 'the right of all nations to complete sovereignty' and expressed its opposition to colonialism in a language that remains apposite: 'With whatever pretexts colonial policies may be justified in the name of religion or civilisation, their sole aim is simply to extend the area of capitalist exploitation in the exclusive interests of the capitalist class.' This was unanimously approved.

---

the world. Some time after the defeat of 1945, Golo Mann wrote of the two Germanies struggling for its soul since its inception. On the one hand 'the Germany of the Kaiser, of the Admiralty, of the General Staff, of Krupp, of self-righteously nationalist Professors, snarling bemonocled lieutenants'. They were confronted by 'the Germany of the great Social-Democratic Party of Bebel and his friends, of Einstein and Planck, of Gerhart Hauptmann'. For him its ultimate collapse was inherent in its founding structures. Bismarck's compromise between the old order of god and king and Junker and liberal bourgeoisie was destined to fail. Might things have been different had it been a republic? The post-Napoleon French imperial example does not inspire much confidence. What is worth noting is the Social Democratic vote prior to the First World War: 27 percent in 1898, 31 percent in 1903, and 35 percent in 1912. But these successes and the much-vaunted tried-and-tested methods of the German SPD were not sufficient to withstand the tide of German nationalism in 1914. And from this tragedy there flowed its successor.

Three years later the British Empire declared war on the Boer Republic in South Africa. The prize was the gold mines of the region. In some ways it was a precursor of the First World War. The Boers were Dutch settlers who had the same colonial 'right' to the territories they occupied as any other power. The interests of the native population were disregarded by both sides. British socialists were horrified by the brutalities and reports of British concentration camps in which the imprisoned Boers were being kept. They organised demonstrations and their newspapers denounced the war as plunder. But this view was by no means unanimous. The Fabian Society defended both the war and the annexation of the Boer territories. Its leading spokesman was the playwright George Bernard Shaw, who made rich claims for the war: it was really a war against slavery and possible genocide; it was being waged to protect the natives of the Transvaal; Britain had to be defended because 'a great power, must, consciously or unconsciously, govern in the general interests of civilization' and any state 'large or small which hinders the spread of international civilization must disappear'.[107] This Fabian tradition was imported whole-sale into the newly created Labour Party, which, whenever it was in office, maintained and preserved the British Empire.

A similar development was taking place in the German Social-Democratic Party. One of its leading intellectuals, Eduard Bernstein, wrote a book in which he criticised the outmoded policy of his party which denounced all acts of imperialism and colonisation as alien to 'the common principles of Social Democracy'.[108] Like the English Fabians, Bernstein argued that, 'Since we enjoy the products of the tropics, why should there be any

---

107 George Bernard Shaw, *Fabianism and the Empire*, Fabian Society, London, 1900. It is sure-ly time for a reprint with a new introduction written by Anthony Giddens and Tony Blair. Shaw's defence of colonial rule created much anger at the time, but he was supported by Sidney and Beatrice Webb and Robert Blatchford, who edited the widely read socialist weekly *Clarion*.
108 Eduard Bernstein, *Die Voraussetzungen des Sozialismus*, Berlin, 1899.

objection to our cultivating the crops ourselves'. And as for 'the right of savages to the soil they occupy', this is not an 'unconditional right'. Why was this the case? Because, 'in the last resort, the higher culture enjoys the higher right. It is not the conquest, but the cultivation of the land that gives the occupier his historical and legal titles.' This was far from being an isolated view. Bernstein received strong support from Gustav Noske, Max Schippel, Ludwig Quessel, and other German equivalents of the British Fabians. But Karl Kautsky and others demolished these views at the party's Mainz Congress in 1900. The view of the overwhelming majority of delegates was that imperialism resulted from 'the insatiable demands of the bourgeoisie to find newer investment outlets for its continually accumulating capital as well as from the drive for new markets'. The delegates insisted that it was the colonial exploiters who became savages in their greed for more wealth and through their oppression of native peoples.

That same year the Second International meeting in Paris unanimously agreed a resolution proposed by Rosa Luxemburg on behalf of the German SPD. She had argued that militarism and colonialism reflected a new development in world politics and economics, a phenomenon whose 'paroxysms had unleashed four bloody wars during the past six years and which threatens the world with a state of permanent war'. The resolution she proposed insisted on a global alliance of workers and the oppressed against the 'world alliance of bourgeoisie and governments'. The latter were for 'perpetual war'. The International would unite people for 'perpetual peace'.

These were fine words, but what would the International do in concrete terms to help the colonial peoples? Here there was no agreement. A special commission on the subject failed to decide on anything conclusive. Some felt that 'it is not necessarily bad for a country to be colonised', others suggested that perhaps in pre-capitalist colonies (i.e. all of them) native forms of capitalism should be encouraged, while a few spoke of the need to develop a 'socialist colonial policy'. The English delegates presented a resolution to a Congress in Amsterdam, which began with the sentence: 'Congress recognises the right of the inhabitants of civilized countries to settle in lands where the population is at a lower stage of development. However it condemns most strongly …', etc.

Nonetheless they all agreed that within colonial rule there should be some degree of self-government, and the entire Congress rose to its feet to applaud the presence of eighty-year-old Dadabhoy Naoroji, the President of the recently formed Indian National Congress.

If this was the level of consciousness of its leaders, what could be expected from the rank-and-file of the European labour movement? Racism, a necessary corollary of Empire, had penetrated deep in the imperialist countries, as the civilisational references in the resolutions presented or discussed at conferences of the Second International reveal. The basis of this racism lay in conquest: We won not because we had the Gatling gun and they did not, but because we were/are a superior race. The colonial moment obscured all other histories. The forward march of competing empires became the dominant narrative. Chinese, Indian, and Islamic civilisations that had governed much of the known world prior to the birth of capitalism in Europe, were forgotten in the Gadarene rush to plant the flag on foreign soil. How could these imperial triumphs in which many workers and peasants had participated directly as soldiers not infect the whole society?

An early demonstration of this came in the 'Hottentot election' in Germany in 1907. The socialists in the Reichstag had voted against war credits to fund a colonial war in South-West Africa, where General von Trotha was busy crushing a rebellion by the native Hereros with the utmost brutality.[109] The Kaiser's parties unleashed a barrage of national-chauvinism

---

109   The battle orders read: 'Within the German borders every Herero, with or without a rifle, with or without cattle, is to be shot. I shall not receive any more women or children;

against the SDP, and in the elections the latter lost half their seats (their number dropping from 81 to 38) and, despite a rise in the number of votes cast, the SPD percentage was down by three points. Bernstein, Noske, and friends attributed this, correctly, to the position taken on Africa. They denounced the 'negative colonial policy' and demanded a more 'realistic and positive' approach. It was this approach that won and led inexorably to the decision that favoured voting in support of war credits in August 1914.

Defeat in war lost Germany its African colonies: Tanganyika was 'mandated' to Britain and South-West Africa to the Union of South Africa. The British Empire, thanks to US intervention in the war, had emerged triumphant. The consequences of this in the Arab east have been discussed in previous chapters.

The Second World War represented both continuity and breach with its predecessor. The continuity was self-evident. Hitler spoke of needing more living space (*Lebensraum*) and ranted endlessly against the British Empire. It is worth reminding ourselves that the war was not fought to 'liberate' the Jews. If that had been the case one would have to acknowledge that it was lost not won. The German fascists, who were handed the German state by a supine bourgeoisie and a decaying aristocracy fearful of Bolshevism, demanded the recognition of Germany as a Great Power. Hitler denounced the British and the French who 'acquired a world by force and robbery' for denying the same rights to the Third Reich:

It cannot be tolerated any longer that the British nation of 44,000,000 souls should remain in possession of fifteen and a half million square miles of the

---

they must be driven back to their people or shot. This is my message to the Hereros – signed Von Trotha, Great General of the Mighty Emperor.' Out of a total population of 80,000, the Great General exterminated 60,000. Such is the power of superior civilisations.

world's surface. They pretend to have obtained it from God and are not prepared to give it away. *Likewise the French nation of 37,000,000 souls owns more than three and a half million square miles, while the German nation with 80,000,000 souls only possesses about 230,000 square miles* [emphasis in original].[110]

Thus, inter-imperialist contradictions were not absent from the causes of the Second World War. Hitler's insistence on receiving the surrender of France in the same rail carriage where the German High Command had been humiliated in 1918 was a symbolic revenge, but one nonetheless designed also to cement the ties between the traditional wing of the army and the Nazi regime.

This second confrontation between the major imperialist powers opened the doors of revolt in the entire colonial world.

The colonial epoch came to end for a variety of reasons. The first of these was the growth of resistance throughout the colonies. This resistance took various forms: armed struggles, non-violent civil disobedience, a combination of the two, the emergence of nationalist political parties, etc. What made this resistance more potent was a wave of social revolutions starting in Russia in 1917 and spreading to China, Korea, Vietnam, and Cuba in the decades that followed. The emergence of this new bloc of anti-capitalist states created a space in which it became less easy to crush the national movements fighting against imperial rule. The nationalist leaders with few exceptions belonged to the educated layers of colonial society. Some had been educated abroad in Britain, France, Portugal, or the Netherlands. They returned home with liberal and radical philosophies and the colonisers realised that if they did not agree to a compromise solution

---

110 *New Order* by Adolf Hitler, cited in Norman Finkelstein, *Image and Reality of the Israel–Palestine Conflict*, new edition, London and New York, 2003, p. 234, footnote 16.

Photograph by REUTERS/Larry Downing

June 2003: the famous golf-cart summit in Egypt after the occupation of Iraq. The Egyptian caddy Hosni Mubarak sits in front while his Saudi counterpart Crown Prince Abdul-Ilah watches from behind. The over-excited unidentified man on the right is trying desperately to stop himself from rising to the occasion.

with the less radical nationalists, the communists would be the only beneficiaries. When forced to choose between a Gandhi or a Ho Chi Minh, the British chose the former. The French decided to struggle till the bitter end. The defeats they suffered in Indo-China and, later, Algeria scarred French society. The Dutch, too, were reluctant to abandon the Indonesian archipelago. The Japanese advance westwards during the Second World War pushed the Dutch and the French out of South-East Asia and strengthened nationalist resistance. After the war both powers, helped by Britain, returned to their colonies, but it was too late. The world had moved on. It was this combination of events that ended the colonial order in the 1960s. As the leader of the capitalist world, the United States now stepped in and attempted to prevent a total collapse. They did so by establishing a chain of military dictatorships in Latin America, Asia, and Africa with two NATO bulwarks (Greece and Turkey) also secured via military regimes. The most bloody representatives of these regimes were Pinochet, Videla, Suharto, and Mobutu, though this short list is not intended as an insult to any of the others, who did their best to maintain the peace. Local resistance was often killed or tortured out of existence.

Readers will, I hope, forgive this long detour. Its purpose is straight-forward. The occupation of Iraq is something new for the younger generations, as most of them are unused to living in countries which dominate others by force, but it is part of a long historical process that was disrupted by the twentieth century and is now back on course. Bush wants Syria and Iran, while his deputy-sheriff in London wants to take over Zimbabwe and Burma (two former British colonies). There is also the question of how Iraq will be ruled in the coming years. The methods of imperial domination are necessarily limited, circumscribed by the existence of a local people with a long history. In the case of Iraq this stretches back three thousand years. Genocide – as applied in the Americas[111] and Australia – is no longer feasible, despite the existence of media barons who would not find it a problem to provide a justification for it.

---

111   The scale of the massacres in South America surprised Charles Darwin. Though he was used to the elimination of animals and plants by stronger species his conversation with a Spanish commander, General Rosas, in 1832 alerted him to the fact that human beings were being exterminated in a similar fashion. The Spanish in Argentina had decided to clear the pampas: 'The Indians are now so terrified that they offer no resistance in a body, but each flies, neglecting even his wife and children; but when overtaken, like wild animals they fight, against any number to the last moment. ... This is a dark picture, but how much more shocking is the undeniable fact that all the women who appear above twenty years old are massacred in cold blood! When I exclaimed that this appeared rather inhuman, he answered "Why, what can be done? They breed so!"' Charles Darwin, *The Voyage of the Beagle*, Chapter 5.

The difference between the United States and the European imperialism of the nineteenth and twentieth centuries is that the former preferred to rule indirectly. Even where they fought major wars – Korea, Vietnam, Angola, Afghanistan – they preferred to be defending local regimes under threat from revolutions rather than ruling directly. Military bases were fine. But a whole apparatus of civilian rule, like that perfected by the British in India, was not Washington's style. When they did occupy a country and administer it, they could be as brutal as the French or the Spanish they were replacing. Two examples suggest themselves: Cuba and the Philippines.

In Cuba, the US helped to defeat the Spaniards, stayed for four years, brought the island's economy under their own control and then departed, leaving behind a semi-independent republic and the military base at Guantanamo Bay, currently being used as the Empire's prison and torture centre.

Benedict Anderson has provided a chilling account of the US occupation and colonisation of the Philippines and its impact on local society.[112] In 1898, President McKinley, encouraged by the press baron Hearst, declared war on Spain in Cuba and the Pacific. The enfeebled Spanish sold their Pacific property to the United States and, as the twentieth century dawned, the 'pacification' of the Philippines began in earnest. The native resistance was not insubstantial. The colonisation cost the United States 5,000 lives, which was all the more painful since the soldiers were overwhelmingly white. Among the Filipinos 20,000 were killed and 200,000 died from starvation and the plague. General Jake Smith, in command of 'pacifying' Samar, gave an order of which General von Trotha would have been proud: 'I want no prisoners. I wish you to kill and burn; the more you burn and kill the better it will please me.' One of his soldiers, a Sergeant Howard McFarlane, wrote to the *Journal* in

---

112 Benedict Anderson, 'Cacique Democracy in the Philippines', in *The Spectre of Comparisons*, London and New York, 2000, pp. 192–226.

Fairfield, Maine: 'On Thursday, March 29 [1900] eighteen of my company killed seventy-five nigger bolomen and ten of the nigger gunners .... When we find one that is not dead, we have bayonets.'[113]

The colonisation of the Philippines ended the semi-autonomy enjoyed by some of the Pacific islands and brought Muslim Mindanao under the control of Manila, with long-term repercussions. On the political front the United States created their own 'oligarchy of racketeers' composed of *mestizo* landowners who were now given the opportunity to buy the 400,000 acres that had been confiscated from the Catholic Church. Yes, when it suited colonial interests, expropriations were permissible. It was all for the greater good. A restricted franchise enabled the oligarchs to dominate their local Congress, and Filipino exports were allowed free, untaxed access through the tariff walls surrounding the United States. The oligarchy flourished, defended by its own private armies, while the majority of the population became even more impoverished. Many from the middle and lower-middle classes, unable to survive or confront the oligarchy, fled to the United States and elsewhere.

Decades later, Ferdinand Marcos destroyed the collective political power of the oligarchs and, with US backing, assumed absolute control, reducing the Philippines to a kleptocracy run by a self-centred, arbitrary, and capricious First Couple. In the countryside a semi-Maoist rural guerrilla movement led by the New People's Army began to garner support and inspire urban disquiet. Their struggle reawakened a popular national consciousness: the depiction of Marcos as an American *tuta* (running dog) became a commonplace on the walls of Manila and in posters in other parts of the country. The scale of corruption and repression led to a massive revolt from below, which was hurriedly commandeered by the

---

113   Ibid. Quoted from Leon Wolff, *Little Brown Brother*, London, 1960, pp. 305 and 360.

army and another oligarchic family. Cory Aquino, *née* Cojuangco, spoke of 'people's power' but was the daughter of the country's leading oligarch, and the rickety coalition of Left and Right that supported her soon collapsed. By 1990 the old pre-Marcos oligarchy of racketeers was firmly back in power. According to the *Philippine Daily Inquirer* survey after the 1987 national elections: 'Out of 200 House representatives, 130 belong to the so-called "traditional political families", while another 39 are relatives of these families. Only 31 Congressmen have no electoral record prior to 1971. ... Of the 24 elected senators ... the cast is largely made up of members of prominent pre-1972 political families.'[114]

There was a symbolic, if unconscious, reference to the status of the islands when in May 2003 the Pentagon announced that Filipino migrants would be transported for menial tasks to the US bases in Iraq. The locals, naturally, have yet to earn their trust.

Which of these fates awaits Iraq? Neither model is particularly suitable. Is the Japanese variant any better? Jackal talk of Iraq becoming like post-war Japan is both irrelevant and ignorant. The question that is currently being discussed by scholars is whether Hirohito of Japan was a war criminal. And if so, why wasn't he tried as such and why did Washington's Viceroy, General Douglas MacArthur, insist on preserving the Chrysanthemum Throne after 1945? Also, contrary to accepted beliefs, there is much evidence to show that hostility to the Emperor-system existed in Japan throughout the 1920s. This denunciation by Uchiyama Gudō, a young priest of the Sōtō Zen sect, should have taught something to the occupying Americans:

> The Big Bullock of the present government, the emperor, is not the
> son of gods as your primary school teachers and others would have

---

114   *Philippine Daily Inquirer*, 24 January 1988.

you believe. The ancestors of the present emperor came forth from a corner of Kyushu, killing and robbing people as they did [so]. They then destroyed their fellow thieves. ... Although this is well-known, university professors and their students, weaklings as they are, refuse to either say or write anything about it. Instead, they attempt to deceive both others and themselves, knowing all along the whole thing is a pack of lies.[115]

Herbert Bix argues that the total involvement of Hirohito with the Japanese war machine and his obsessive desire for imperial expansion was always well known in Japan. A gigantic cover-up and sanitisation process was necessary in order to keep him on the throne. Hirohito was busy preparing his defence for the War Crimes Tribunal when he was informed that this would not be necessary.[116]

None of these examples would suit the recolonisation of Iraq. Time could certainly be bought by a version of the Marshall Plan, which

---

115   Quoted in *Hirohito and the Making of Modern Japan* by Herbert P. Bix, London, 2000. This insightful volume by a leading scholar should be required reading for Iraqi quislings who idealise this particular occupation.

116   General MacArthur and his colleague Brigadier General Fellers were determined to shield Hirohito from the very moment their plane landed in Japan. Both men were violently anti-radical, regarding President Roosevelt and the New Deal in their own country as a crypto-commie plot. In addition, Fellers was notoriously anti-Semitic, calmly informing the Japanese High Command that the top adviser to Secretary of State Byrnes was 'Cohen (a Jew and a communist) ... the most influential advocate of un-American thought in the United States'.

On 6 March 1946, Fellers summoned Admiral Yonai Mitsumasa and his interpreter Mizota Shuichi and informed them that the Soviet Union and some other Allied countries were insisting that Hirohito be punished as a war criminal. Fellers suggested that:

'To counter this situation, it would be most convenient if the Japanese side could prove to us that the emperor is completely blameless. I think the forthcoming trials offer the best opportunity to do that. Tojo, in particular, should be made to bear all the responsibility at his trial. In other words, I want you to have Tojo say as follows: "At the imperial conference prior to the start of war, I had already decided to push for war even if His Majesty the Emperor was against going to war with the United States."' Ibid.

immediately proceeds to rebuild the destroyed infrastructure, provide subsidised housing and other facilities and permit the Iraqi people to elect their own parliament. But the system of domination in force at the moment is not the New Deal but neo-liberal economics, which makes doing in Iraq what you dare not do at home a difficult operation, since it violates the rules of the World Trade Organisation/International Monetary Fund, which are crucial to maintaining tooth-and-claw capitalism in power elsewhere. Democracy creates further problems as it did in Iran in 1953. What if the Iraqis elect a government that insists on keeping oil under Iraqi control and demand the withdrawal of the occupation armies and US bases. It might not happen immediately, but the medium-term possibility is always present. That would necessitate another regime change.

These are the problems that now confront the Empire and they will become even more pressing if the US moves in the direction of Iran. The more intelligent of the mainstream political analysts in the United States are much more aware of this than the ostrich-liberals who refuse to accept the reality of what confronts them.

In a recent book, Andrew J. Bacevich, a former military officer, now Professor of International Relations at Boston University, refusing to accept that the Bush administration represents any serious breach with the Clinton or Bush Sr years, raises a number of significant questions. The 'dirty little secret' of the Bush–Clinton–Bush years is the refusal to admit the scale of the imperial problem:

> Holding sway in not one but several regions of pivotal geopolitical importance, disdaining the legitimacy of political economic principles other than its own, declaring the existing order to be sacrosanct, asserting unquestioned military supremacy with a globally deployed force configured not for self-defense but for coercion: these are the actions of a nation engaged in the governance of empire. Continuing

to pretend otherwise – in the words of Reinhold Niebuhr, 'frantically avoiding recognition of the imperialism we in fact exercise' – won't make America's imperial problem any easier to manage and certainly won't make it go away. [117]

Every empire has, sooner or later, provoked a reaction. Whenever a despot – indigenous or proconsular – realises that nothing works any more, that the torture and misery he has inflicted on his subjects is not enough to save him, he becomes more and more paranoid. The false smiles of his advisers no longer deceive him. Underneath the mask on each and every face he can read the expectation of his decline and doom. That is why astrologers in the East usually predicted misfortune to all those who entered the service of a tyrant. The armed resistance in Iraq has been discussed earlier, but what of the political opposition to the Empire?

For a whole decade the *bien-pensants* and left-of-centre governments have sought to avoid the reality of US power by taking cover under the flimsy umbrella of the United Nations. The Empire was fine provided it consulted the Security Council or, at the very minimum, NATO. It was imperial unilateralism that was unacceptable. Or, as the much-esteemed German philosopher Jurgen Habermas wrote after the fall of Baghdad: 'Let us not close our eyes before this revolution in world affairs: the normative authority of America lies shattered.' [118]

The arguments deployed by Habermas and others are important because they represent a significant sector of West European public

---

117   Andrew J. Bacevich, *American Empire: The Realities and Consequences of US Diplomacy*, Harvard, 2002, pp. 243–4.
118   Jurgen Habermas, 'What does the felling of the monument mean?', *Frankfurter Allgemeine Zeitung*, 17 April 2003.

opinion. This view can be summarised as follows. The imposition of Western liberal hegemony is only justifiable if it conforms with international law. Pragmatists and opportunists in Europe, who are now bowing before accomplished facts and accepting the war in Iraq, are mistaken. The universalist core of democracy and the values attached to it contradict imperial demands that impose uniformity. The only way to curb unilateralist excesses is through the only existing world organisation and to further the development of international law, before which all are equal. If this is not done, the rule of law will suffer globally, and inside the United States it is already being undermined by the powers granted to the security services. And pre-empting comparisons with the Yugoslav war, Habermas writes:

> The comparison with the intervention in Kosovo also offers no exoneration. It is true that an authorisation by the Security Council in this case was not reached either. But the retrospectively obtained legitimation could be based on three circumstances: on the prevention – as it seemed at the time – of an ethnic cleansing in the process of taking place, on the imperative – covered by international law – of emergency assistance holding *erga omnes* for this case, as well as the incontrovertibly democratic and constitutional character of all the member states of the ad hoc military alliance.[119]

In other words, the Iraq war of 2003 was completely different in character. In response to Jurgen Habermas, one could pose a set of alternative questions. Given that US defiance of the UN constitutes the main argument against the war (this was the soft underbelly of the European peace movement) and Security Council approval a sanction of

---

119   Habermas, op cit.

international law, let us see if we can unravel this problem. Does the United Nations Security Council constitute the Supreme Court of international law? If so, how can it implement some resolutions and not others. The UN and its predecessor, the League of Nations, were created to institutionalise the new status quo arrived at after two bloody conflicts – the First and Second World Wars. Both organisations were founded on the understanding that they would defend the right of nations to self-determination. In both cases their charters outlawed pre-emptive strikes and any attempts to occupy countries or change regimes. Both organisations suggested that the nation state had replaced empires.[120]

The UN was created to police the Yalta Accords after the defeat of fascism. Its charter expressly prohibits the violation of national sovereignty except in the case of 'self-defence'. However, despite the presence of the Soviet Union, the UN was unable to defend the newly independent Congo against Belgian and US intrigue in the 1960s or to save the life of the Congolese leader Patrice Lumumba. And in 1950 the Security Council took advantage of a temporary Soviet boycott to authorise a US war in Korea. Under the UN banner the Western armies deliberately destroyed dams, power stations, and the infrastructure of social life in North Korea, plainly in breach of international law. The UN was also unable to stop the war in Vietnam. Its paralysis over the occupation of Palestine has been visible for over three decades. Nor was this masterly inactivity restricted to Western abuses. The UN was powerless to defend Hungary against the Soviet invasion (1956) or Czechoslovakia against the Warsaw Pact's decision to change the regime

---

120   The League of Nations collapsed soon after the Italian fascists occupied Ethiopia. Mussolini defended his invasion of Albania and Abyssinia by arguing that he was removing the 'corrupt, feudal and oppressive regime' of King Zog/Haile Selassie and Italian news-reels showed grateful Albanians/Ethiopeans applauding the entry of Italian troops. And of European civilisation?

of that country (1968). Both Big Powers were, in other words, allowed to do their business in clear breach of the UN charter and without incurring sanctions.

With the US as the only military-imperial state, the Security Council today has become a venue for trading not insults, but a share of the loot. The Italian theorist most feared by the fascists of the last century predicted this turn of events with amazing prescience. 'The "normal" exercise of hegemony,' wrote Antonio Gramsci, 'is characterised by the combination of force and consent, in variable equilibrium, without force predominating too much over consent.' There were, Gramsci elaborated, occasions when it was more appropriate to resort to a third variant of hegemony, because 'between consent and force stands corruption-fraud, that is the enervation and paralysing of the antagonist or antagonists'.[121] Here we have an exact description of the process used to try and win Russian support at the UN as revealed in a front-page headline in the *Financial Times* (4 October 2002): 'Putin drives hard bargain with US over Iraq's oil: Moscow wants high commercial price for its support'.

European allies shuffle their feet at excessive US 'unilateralism' – essentially this is a discomfiting failure to consult, which serves as a cover for European subordination. China and Russia bargain weakly in return for their favours in the Security Council. If these are not forthcoming, action is taken anyway.

The world has changed so much over the last two decades that the UN has become an anachronism, a permanent fig leaf for new imperial adventures. If it was genuinely representative of the present world order, it would have only one veto in the Security Council, that of the United States. Boutros Boutros-Ghali was sacked on Madeline Albright's insistence

---

121   Perry Anderson, 'Force and Consent', *New Left Review* 17, September/October 2002.

for challenging the imperial will: he had insisted that it was the Rwandan genocide that needed intervention. US interests required a presence in the Balkans. He was replaced by the current incumbent. Kofi Annan is a weak placeman whose sanctimonious speeches may sometimes deceive an innocent European public, but not himself. He knows who calls the shots. He knows who provides the song-sheet. And the same United Nations provided retrospective sanction to the occupation of Iraq.[122] That is why some (including the author) insisted that a UN-backed war would be as immoral and unjust as the one that was plotted by the Pentagon, because it would have been the same war. Likewise, the character of the Anglo-American occupation will not change simply because the Security Council has given it approval. All that does is bring the EU and some others (Lula in Brazil, Musharraf in Pakistan, Vajpayee in India, etcetera) back into line.

Jurgen Habermas and European public opinion was fully prepared to accept that the UN could be ignored in Yugoslavia because the 'ad-hoc alliance' which made war on that occasion consisted exclusively of 'democratic states'. But surely the Anglo-American alliance that captured Iraq is equally democratic. Bush and Blair are elected leaders. Even if doubt is cast on Bush's own election, what is clear is that he had the virtually unanimous support of both Senate and Congress as well as the Democratic Party, whose two biggest draws, Mr and Mrs Clinton, played an important role in rallying public opinion in favour of the war. Why should the fact that important democratic states in Europe

---

122   In a posthumous, but prescient, text, published in *Harper's Monthly* in 1916, Mark Twain described the processes well: 'Next the statesmen will invent cheap lies, putting the blame upon the nation that is attacked, and every man will be glad of those conscience-soothing falsities, and will diligently study them, and refuse to examine any refutations of them; and thus he will by and by convince himself that the war is just, and will thank God for the better sleep he enjoys after this process of grotesque self-deception.'

(Germany, France, Belgium) opposed the war before it took place nullify the criteria.

The contrast with Yugoslavia is not as profound as imagined by Habermas. In fact those who 'invoke humanity' could argue that Saddam Hussein's regime was much worse than any of the post-1990 Balkan outfits. True, there was nothing to see on the TV screen, no bad images to mobilise the public, but that should not invalidate the argument. The same 'surgical precision' that was applauded in Yugoslavia was deployed in Iraq. Civilian casualties were relatively low. And the same Kantian reasoning applied in this case. This time, of course, when faced with a 'blocked Security Council' and a blocked NATO, the United States decided to go ahead anyway and would have done so even without Blair. That much has become clear.[123] In a recent intervention, Habermas and Jacques Derrida have published a joint appeal for an independent European foreign policy. What policy? Which Europe? Unless the reality of US imperial power is understood it is difficult to mount a political challenge. Within the United States itself there are Empire loyalists who fear isolation. For them institutions such as the UN and NATO are useful devices to maintain a consensual Western hegemony and should not be treated in a cavalier fashion.[124] They have been used in the past and will be again.

---

123   Danilo Zolo, *Invoking Humanity: War, Law and Global Order*, London and New York, 2002. This is one of the most effective critiques of 'humanitarian interventionism'.

124   The most recent version of this argument is provided by Joseph S. Nye, 'US Power and Strategy After Iraq', in *Foreign Affairs*, July/August 2003. Nye accepts the basic continuity in US foreign policy since Woodrow Wilson, but has these words of advice: 'Both the neo-Wilsonian and the Jacksonian strands of the new unilateralism tend to prefer alliance a la carte and to treat international institutions as toolboxes into which US policymakers can reach when convenient. But this approach neglects the ways in which institutions legitimize disproportionate American power. When others feel they have been consulted, they are more likely to be helpful.'

And if Europe's left-liberal intellectuals and philosophers still doubt that the world in which we live is dominated by a single empire and its needs, one might suggest that they read Philip Bobbitt's impassioned defence of the US Empire. A Democrat himself, Bobbitt is a transatlantic academic with positions in Austin (Texas), Oxford, and Kings College, London, and has served four US Presidents in various capacities: Carter, Reagan, Bush the father, and Clinton, the last as Director of Intelligence on the National Security Council. Prior to and during the war on Iraq, Bobbitt became a familiar figure in Blairite Britain, fêted in the media and a regular visitor to 10 Downing Street. In other words, this is a man with some authority. What does his latest book tell us?

Its message is upbeat. A Bismarckian revolution is underway in international relations and it was launched not by George W., but by Bill Clinton when he decided to intervene in the Balkans. Whatever the merits or demerits of the case, this intervention overrode traditional attitudes to national sovereignty in the name of humanity. In an interview with the *Guardian* after the occupation of Iraq, Bobbitt boasted of how it was he who had convinced Clinton of the need for a new doctrine to justify imperial policies in the post-communist world:

> The US would intervene when the threat to our vital strategic interests was overwhelming and imminent; or when significant strategic interests and humanitarian concerns coincided; or, when a vital strategic interest was absent, humanitarian concerns were high and strategic interests were low.[125]

---

125   *Guardian*, 7 June 2003. The book is *The Shield of Achilles: War, Peace, and the Course of History*, by Philip Bobbitt, New York, 2002. For a devastating indictment of this work see Gopal Balakrishnan, 'Achilles Shield and the Market State', in *New Left Review* 23, September/October 2003.

This aggressive agenda is now in place and one important reason to recognise the 'disproportionate power' of the American Empire is to aid the development of a political resistance and a proper alternative. The movement that is needed can only be effective if it is global; and if it understands that the neo-liberal legs on which the imperial giant walks are not as strong as capitalist witch-doctors like to suggest.

APPENDIX:
CHRISTOPHER HITCHENS AND THE FIRST GULF WAR

Once upon a time there was a radical English journalist. Despite harbouring a crush on Margaret Thatcher (his little secret), he tired of life on the sceptred isle. Who can blame him? His huge talents, not to mention a watermelon-sized ego, could not be confined to an increasingly provincial medium-sized country in Northern Europe. He decided to shift continents. When he arrived in New York in the 1980s, my old friend and comrade, Alexander Cockburn, already established there as a writer and columnist, introduced the new arrival to New York society. Cockburn has barred me from writing of those early years. The more delicious morsels are being saved for his own memoirs. The crumbs offered me are too tasteless for a book of this sort, which I hope will be read by many old people. So I fast-forward.

Soon afterwards, Christopher H. began to write a regular column, 'Minority Report', for *The Nation*, a radical New York weekly. It appeared every fortnight and was a good column, even when one disagreed with its contents. It was often witty and unpredictable, except when the author adopted an unpleasant tone (shades of the future) towards anyone even mildly critical of George Orwell or Salman Rushdie, or anyone else Hitchens had positioned on his own private pedestal. Pity the columnist who needs heroes.

Ten years ago, however, bullying outbursts were rare. The battle for Christopher H.'s soul – fought over by two veterans of, respectively, Greek mythology and the Old Testament – had not yet begun in earnest. Occasionally in his writing, one could detect the friendly sparring between Narcissus and Onan, but in the main, it must be admitted, radical politics were in command. He had something to say. And he said it well.

During the First Gulf War, Hitchens posed some searching and pertinent questions. Since they are even more relevant today, it's worth alerting a younger generation to their value given that most see the journalist as he is now – a permanently flushed, reactionary bruiser, a 'warmonger who sells war, like a fishmonger sells fish', to quote Sir Rodric Braithwaite's description of Tony Blair. It was not always thus.

Early on in the crisis, the anti-imperialist Hitchens questioned the West's obsession with Kuwait and declared his sympathy for the Iraqi position:

> It is certainly possible for the United States to reconquer the whole of Kuwait if it chooses to do so, but such an outcome would only restore an untenable status quo. When the British drew the borders they did so with the specific intention of denying Iraq access to the sea, and thus of making it more dependent on Britain. Sir Anthony Parsons, former foreign policy adviser to Margaret Thatcher, former envoy to the United Nations and hardened veteran of the region, put it like this only last month: 'In the Iraqi subconscious, Kuwait is part of Basra province, and the bloody British took it away from them. We protected our strategic interests rather successfully, but in doing so we didn't worry too much about the people living there. We created a situation where people felt they had been wronged.' (*The Nation*, 2 October 1990)

Hitchens goes on to denounce those who talk of 'appeasement' and to argue that a compromise solution is necessary. Possibly Kuwait could be leased to Iraq – with or without the ruling family – and the West should pressure Kuwait in this direction. But there is a more pressing problem:

> The danger at the moment is that President Bush, flush with his triumphs on the international stage, will seek to overthrow Saddam and also to create some permanent nexus of alliances in the region. It would be fascinating to know if he has any idea who ought to run Iraq, and it would also be interesting to know how long he would commit himself to the task. The Israeli Right seems to take the view that no Arab state should be allowed to evolve beyond a certain level of strength and development; thus Carthage needs to be levelled every decade or so. Is this to be Washington's policy also? (*The Nation*, 2 October 1990)

A fortnight later, Hitchens quoted Albert Einstein denouncing Menachim Begin as 'a fascist' in the '*New York Times* in 1948' (why didn't the renowned *Nation* fact-checkers get him the exact date?), and informed his readers of his own distaste for the Israeli winner of a Nobel Peace Prize. He went on to defend Patrick Buchanan ('a solid home-grown McCarthyite with proto-fascist tendencies') who had been labelled a Nazi 'because he doesn't care for the influence of Yitzhak Shamir – the only living politician in the Middle East who actually offered himself as a volunteer for the Hitler side in World War II'. The column ended with a witty denunciation of Martin Peretz of *The New Republic*. His crime? He had called for Iraq to be captured and dismembered.

Soon it was time for a little general-bashing:

> When I saw the low-comedy figure of General H. Norman Schwarzkopf Jr. swim onto my screen the other day, talking out of the side of his mouth about 'kicking the butt' of Saddam Hussein and beaming at the puerile appellation 'Stormin' Norman' a rat stirred in the cluttered attic

of my memory. I knew of course that the general had covered himself in glory in Vietnam and Grenada. But wasn't there something else familiar about the name? (*The Nation*, 29 October 1990)

Of course there was, and readers were duly told that Norm's dad had done dirty work in Iran for the CIA and helped topple a democratic regime which had nationalised the country's oil industry in 1952: 'Stormin' Norman clearly is not genetically responsible for his father's role in helping pick a Hitler fan to govern Iran. Yet this father–son gendarmerie for the oil industry is better seen as continuity than coincidence.' And, incidentally, the military intervention in Iraq was a sign of 'imperial decay' because the US could not solve the crisis in any other way. In November 1990, readers of the column were informed of the similarities between the Sabah family in Kuwait and the Bush clan in the US. Both were involved in dodgy deals, and Hitchens quite properly asked: 'Are the Bushes worth dying for?' His answer: 'Not worth dying for, I'd say. Not worth killing for either.' Why not? Because President Bush and his sons were up to no good. Neil Bush was facing charges of improper conduct; Jeb Bush was being bailed out of trouble with government cash to the tune of $4.6 million; and, yes:

> In this delicious world dwells also George Bush Jr., the eldest son of our all-wise Chief Exec and a 'director, large stock-holder, and $120,000-a-year consultant to a Texas oil company whose potentially lucrative drilling rights in the Persian Gulf are being protected by American troops.' I am quoting from the invaluable Pete Brewton of *The Houston Post*, who broke the initial S&L story ... (*The Nation*, 12 November 1990)

Three months later, as Operation Desert Storm is about to commence, Hitchens indicts the President, George Herbert Walker Bush, for numerous crimes, including a refusal to take seriously a last-minute bid for peace by several countries and the UN Secretary-General. Hitchens is very stern on the question of Palestine. Bush is accused of using Israeli military and intelligence facilities to plan the war. Later we are told that whereas in the past there was some cosmetic commitment to settling the 'essential, central, defining question of Palestine', now it's 'goodbye to all that'. The very next column is Hitchens at his mocking best, denouncing the crude use of Churchilliana to bolster the resident at the White House and the denunciation of all enemies as being morally equivalent to Hitler. As the US goes to war, *The Nation* columnist from somewhere on high calmly pours vitriol on the President's head.

On 11 March 1991 there is a tough-minded denunciation of Western racism, the 'coarsening of domestic public opinion', and the 'cretinisation of the media', all of which, like much else in these columns, is even more apposite in 2003, and for that reason, personal pronoun notwithstanding, deserves to be quoted in full:

On December 28 last, I pulled a long face as I cut out and kept a front-page story by the Washington bureau chief of the *Los Angeles Times*, the sagacious and well-connected Jack Nelson. The article concerned the coming war, as it would be fought at home. It reported a conversation with 'two officials involved with Bush in Persian Gulf strategy'. I cut it out because I thought I might be needing it: 'The officials said Bush assumes the American public will be mainly concerned about the number of US casualties, not the tens of thousands of Iraqis who stand to die or be maimed in a massive air assault, and that even the killing of thousands of civilians – including women and children – probably would not undermine American support for the war effort.'

As I write, the opinion polls show that a well-fed public believes there was a mass suicide in a Baghdad bunker, orchestrated with the fell purpose of making George look, and Barbara feel, bad. This filthy plot, which unfolded just a day short of qualifying to call itself the St. Valentine's Day Provocation, was thwarted by American resolve. Three days before it, Dick Cheney and Colin Powell were photographed as they wrote jaunty inscriptions on the casings of about-to-be-used bombs. In the hours after it, Marlin Fitzwalter opined solemnly that certain Iraqis had a different attitude toward death. (Do you notice that this usually means that the speaker has a different attitude towards the death of Iraqis?) … To possess an empire, it is necessary to be tough and resilient. The public must in principle be ready at all times to display an unflinching stoicism, a stern willingness to endure the suffering of complete strangers. Without this resolute quality, the entire concept of 'peace through strength' would become a hollow thing …

Two weeks later the war is over. Between 50,000 and 100,000 Iraqi soldiers have died in vain. Hitchens leaves it to the Iraqis to determine how many of these deaths are due to Saddam Hussein. For him the decision to kill the soldiers of a retreating army, after its offer to withdraw under international supervision and its acceptance of UN Resolution 660 has been rejected, is imperialist immorality at its worst:

I look forward to editions of *Sesame Street* and other special programming in place of cartoon fare in which American children will have the turkey shoot explained to them. I look forward to more statements from American peaceniks explaining how it is that they support the troops but not the war. I especially look forward to fresh Augustinian tautologies from our churchmen about proportionality in a just war. But perhaps we may be relieved of the necessity for these reassurances. After all, if no misgivings are expressed, where is the need for rationalization? (*The Nation*, 25 March 1991)

The triumphalism and the gloating that follow the war angers Hitchens. He writes:

> Over the past several weeks I have been intrigued by the non-existence of the phrase 'the Mutlaa massacre'. Mutlaa is the site of the funkily named 'Highway of Death' where American pilots caught a convoy of fleeing Iraqis, bombed the vehicles at both ends and then returned to shred and dismember the resulting traffic jam again and again. Everybody sat and watched *those* pictures. ... If everybody who marvelled at the absence of a protest had protested, there would have been a protest …
>
> Not one voice is being raised to inquire what the United States Army is now doing in Iraq. ... Meanwhile, Palestinian agriculture on the West Bank has been all but destroyed by a curfew that has prevented the tending of fields or animals. ... In an attempt to split the PLO, Saudi and Kuwaiti envoys have met in Damascus with Ahmed Jibril and Abu Musa, two mercenary puppets with rejectionist records. Iran is gloating at the Lebanonisation of Iraq, a process that the US occupation is apparently not designed to retard. All the tactics of divide-and-rule, of the sort that led to the war in the first place, are being pursued with great vigour. And we … look on. (*The Nation*, 8 April 1991)

Anger continued to mount. Bush was both 'Desert Stormtrooper' and 'Desert Rat'. The bombing of Iraq was compared to that of Dresden and Hitchens insisted that Western leaders and their local puppets be brought before a war crimes tribunal after the war. His reasons for this were cogent and compelling:

> Bear in mind what Bush and his 'people' have done. They have smashed the civilian infrastructure of an entire country, deliberately tearing apart

the web of water, electricity and sewage lines that held it together. They have killed at least 100,000 conscripts (neatly sparing the 'elite Republican Guard' in order to conform to Saudi wishes) and a vast, uncounted number of non-combatants. They have prepared the way for the next wave of Apocalyptic horsemen in the form of famine and pestilence, described chillingly in reports from the UN and the International Red Cross. Their forces continue to occupy territory in Iraq ... (*The Nation*, 6 May 1991)

And in his last column on the war, after accusing General Schwarzkopf of violating the US Constitution by accepting an honour from the English Queen, he turned on the 'many liberals and even leftists who, during the run-up to the conflict, pronounced themselves co-belligerents. A popular formulation was "I prefer imperialism to fascism". Now with a ruined Iraq and a strengthened Saddam – not to mention a strengthened al-Saud and Sabah – we no longer have to choose between imperialism and fascism, we can have both.'

The situation in Iraq and the region (especially Palestine) is much worse in 2003 than it was in 1991. The iron heel of Zionism is firmly embedded on the neck of Palestine. Iraq is occupied by troops under command of a man whose father Hitchens wanted tried for war crimes. British troops are back in Basrah. In 1991 the infrastructure was repaired by the Iraqi regime within two months of the conclusion of hostilities. But at least water and electricity were restored within three weeks. They are still not available at the time of writing, nearly three months after the taking of Baghdad. Had it not been for the sanctions following the First Gulf War, Iraq might have returned to its pre-war condition in terms of health and education.

These days, Christopher Hitchens describes himself as 'a consultant to the White House'. If only the Clintons had done the decent thing and invited him during their tenure, they might have avoided his ferocious attacks on them. What happened to him? On 11 September 2001, a small group of terrorists crashed the planes they had hijacked into the Pentagon and the Twin Towers of New York. It was a terrible tragedy. Among the casualties, though unreported that week, was a middle-aged *Nation* columnist by the name of Christopher Hitchens. He was never seen again. The vile replica currently on offer is a double.[126]

---

126   Though not according to his old friend and protégé, Dennis Perrin, who wrote a long farewell in the *Minneapolis City Paper* on 9 July 2003. He's sure it's the same guy alright and concludes his essay thus:

I can barely read him anymore. His pieces in the Brit tabloid The Mirror and in Slate are a mishmash of imperial justifications and plain bombast; the old elegant style is dead.

His TV appearances show a smug, nasty scold with little tolerance for those who disagree with him. He looks more and more like a Ralph Steadman sketch. And in addition to all this, he's now revising what he said during the buildup to the Iraq war.

In several pieces, including an incredibly condescending blast against Nelson Mandela, Hitch went on and on about WMD, chided readers with 'Just you wait!' and other taunts, fully confident that once the US took control of Iraq, tons of bio/chem weapons and labs would be all over the cable news nets – with him dancing a victory jig in the foreground. Now he says WMD were never a real concern, and that he'd always said so. It's amazing that he'd dare state this while his earlier pieces can be read at his website. But then, when you side with massive state power and the cynical fucks who serve it, you can say pretty much anything and the People Who Matter won't care.

Currently, Hitch is pushing the line, in language that echoes the reactionary Paul Johnson, that the US can be a 'superpower for democracy,' and that Toms Jefferson and Paine would approve. He's also slammed the 'slut' Dixie Chicks as 'fucking fat slags' for their rather mild critique of our Dear Leader. He favors Bush over Kerry, and doesn't like it that Kerry 'exploits' his Vietnam combat experience (as opposed to, say, re-election campaign stunts on aircraft carriers).

Sweet Jesus. What next? I'm afraid my old mentor is not the truth-telling Orwell he fancies himself to be. He's becoming a coarser version of Norman Podhoretz.

INDEX